D0368196

Coastal Ghosts

OTHER BOOKS BY NANCY RHYNE:

The Grand Strand: An Uncommon Guide to
Myrtle Beach and Its Surroundings

Carolina Seashells

Tales of the South Carolina Low Country

More Tales of the South Carolina Low Country

Murder in the Carolinas

Once Upon a Time on a Plantation

Plantation Tales

More Murder in the Carolinas

Alice Flagg

Touring the Coastal South Carolina Backroads

Coastal Ghosts

HAUNTED PLACES
FROM WILMINGTON, NORTH CAROLINA
TO SAVANNAH, GEORGIA

Nancy Rhyne

Sandlapper Publishing, Inc.
Orangeburg, South Carolina

MSU LIBRARY - ARCH

© 1985 by Fast & McMillan Publishers, Inc.
© 1989 by Nancy Rhyne

All rights reserved. This book may not be reproduced, in whole
or in part, in any form (except by reviewers for the public press),
without written permission from the publisher.

MANUFACTURED IN THE UNITED STATES OF AMERICA

ISBN 0-87844-049-6 (PB)   ISBN 0-87844-092-5 (HB)

Library of Congress in Publication Data

Rhyne, Nancy. 1926–
Coastal ghosts.

Includes index.

1. Atlantic States – Description and travel – Guide-books. 2. Legends – Atlantic
States. 3. Ghosts – Atlantic States. 4. Atlantic Coats (United States) –
Description and travel – Guide-books. 5. Plantations – Atlantic States – Guide-
books.

I. Title.

F207.3.R49   917.5 85-71258

Sandlapper Publishing, Inc., Orangeburg, South Carolina
4 5 6 7 8 9 10   92 93 94 95 96 97 98 99

Acknowledgments

I most gratefully acknowledge the following people, without whose help this manuscript would never have evolved into a finished work:

Beverly Tetterton of the New Hanover County Library; Harry Warren, Researcher, New Hanover County Museum; George E. Harrill, son of the Hermit; Dr. James A. Lanier, Marine Resources Center, Fort Fisher; Clarke A. Willcox of Murrells Inlet; our good friend Edwin O. Fulton of Wachesaw Plantation; the late Genevieve Willcox Chandler; Wynness Thomas; Robert H. Joyner of the Tom Yawkey Wildlife Center; Robert Mitchell, Superintendent of Hampton Plantation State Park; Will Alston of Hampton Plantation; Charles P. Dooling, Deputy Public Affairs Officer, Navy Charleston; PHAN Mike Mummert, Naval Base, Charleston; the Reverend Doctor Robert E. H. Peeples, President, Hilton Head Island Historical Society; Helen Amsdorff, Savannah Area Convention and Visitors Bureau; Herb Traub of Pirates' House; Chris Jurgenson of 17 Hundred 90; Gloria Nanfria, Bonnie Gueller, Bill Royal, Rebecca, and the others at The Olde Pink House Restaurant & Planters Tavern, Savannah.

Last but not least, Sid Rhyne, my better half, who assisted me in all facets of this project.

For Sid

Contents

Prologue 9
North Carolina 15
    About Wilmington 17
        Wilmington's Haunted House on Market Street 19
        The Strange Burial of Nancy Martin 25
        The Man Who Was Buried Alive 33
        The Eradication of the Hermit 39
South Carolina 45
    The Grand Strand 47
        Alice Flagg 49
        The Curse of the Wachesaw Skulls 55
        Theodosia Burr 61
        Doctor Flagg 67
        The Ghost of the Crab Boy 71
        A Bride, a Groom and a Church Full of Ghosts 77
    Georgetown 85
        The Headless Sentry 87
        The Man Who Turned To Stone 93
        A Sinking Feeling 99
    Hampton Plantation 105
        The Hampton Ghost 107
        The Sweetest Legend of Hampton 113
    Charleston 117
        The Ghost in St. Philips Graveyard 119
        The Ghost at Charleston's City Hall 127
        The Haunted Avenue of Oaks 133

Hilton Head Island....................................139
   The Eliza Tree 141
   The Unparalleled Rides of the Late William Baynard 149
Daufuskie Island 155
   Daufuskie's Big Foot............................157
Georgia..161
   Savannah 163
   Savannah's Sweetheart of Mankind 165
   The Ghost at the Pirate's House.....................171
   The Ghost of Mr. Habersham 175
   17 Hundred 90 181
Epilogue 185
Index..187

Prologue

"Do you believe in ghosts?" As I sit in bookstores, autographing books, that is the question asked of me more often than any other. To tell you the truth, I don't know how I feel about ghosts, but I've witnessed some happenings that were not explainable, and I have talked with some well-educated, highly respected people who told me they have encountered ghosts. I have found no reason not to believe them.

I'll never forget the glamorous young woman who stood before me in a Charleston department store, holding an armful of books to be inscribed to members of her family. Sophisticated, right out of the *Town & Country* set, she had been brought up on a plantation on the May River, near Beaufort, South Carolina. "I cannot explain this," she said, "but all of my life we heard parties going on in that house. We heard music, much laughing, and taffeta rustled as ladies twirled and stepped into dances. I can't explain it, but *I heard it.*"

And there was the day that I was in the All Saints Church burial ground, near Pawleys Island, and a woman came up to me and started talking about ghosts. "I can tell you this," she began. "My sister died, and I was so worried about her daughter, who was about to marry a man of questionable character. The whole family was anxious about that marriage, and we all begged the girl not to go through with it. Then, one day, my deceased sister came to me. She walked right through a closed door, and I remember it explicitly. I can visualize right now the dress she was wearing. She soothingly suggested that I worry no more about her daughter, and she told me that the marriage would turn out to be a successful one. That was several years ago. My niece married the man, and no other man in the world could be a better husband for her."

Robert Mitchell, Superintendent of Hampton Plantation State Park, says he has heard strange goings-on there, and he believes he's heard the famous "Big Foot of the West" during a hunting expedition. William Starr, cultural affairs editor of the *State* (published in Columbia, it's the largest newspaper in South Carolina) wrote that he has seen the Gray Man, Pawleys Island's most famous ghost. Nate Shulimson, owner of the Book Shoppe on Restaurant Row in Myrtle Beach, has talked about seeing a ghost in a college dormitory.

If ghosts and other weird critters really do exist, what more appropriate place for their habitat than the Low Country of the Carolinas and Georgia. An ancient woman named Addie, her clothes hanging on her skeletonlike frame like a scarecrow, her hair plaited down and tightly wrapped with white twine framing a face webbed with wrinkles, said, "There was a critter named plat-eye. They takes the shape of all kind of critter — dog, cat, hog, mule, varmint, and I even hear tell of plat-eye taking form of gator."

One of Addie's friends talked about Low Country creatures: "They's hants and they's ghosts. And a plat-eye some of those ole timey people sees. Ghost just be an evil spirit. Most of them creatures be hants, hags, plat-eye or ghosts."

If the people who lived on the back roads of the South Carolina Low Country felt one of the creatures from the outer world was nearby even though they could not see it, the effect it produced was often worse than if it had been clearly visible.

The malevolent influence was always felt, and a sort of numbness would creep over the victim.

> It was worser than a bad dream, cause you
> can't wake up. Your hair tauten and you gets
> cold. Me! I ain't ever going through them
> woods since that thing frighten me. No, suh. I
> could tell when I near the creature what been
> in there. Me skin be prickly, and the flesh
> crawl on the back of my neck. It been Saturday
> night and while the water hotten for me bath,
> I read me Bible. Course you know I can't right-
> ly read, but I could hold the book and look at
> the page and say some of the verse I hear in
> church. The whole time I wash, I been think-
> ing how good the bed gonna feel. I put on a
> clean gown, and outen the light, then I step in
> the bed. When I stretch out to enjoy the feel, I
> clare to God, iffen a pin didn't rake the whole
> side of me leg. That debbil of a ghost put em
> there.

It's difficult to pin someone down on whether they really believe in ghosts. But, as Addie says, "This is the land where when the sun goes down and it becomes dusky dark, you see all kinds of varmint, plat-eye, hants, hags and ghosts. In this land the moccasin lashes the rushes, and the moss is low, and the cooter lives, and the firefly flickers, and when a bull frog hits the water, it goes *kerplunk*. Yes," says Addie, "you have to learn how to fend them off. Plat-eye can't stand the smell of gun powder and sulphur mixed. So I totes my powder and sulphur and carries my stick in my hand, and puts my trust in the Lord."

The presence of ghosts has long been cited in literature.

Shakespeare seats a ghost in a particular chair in the banquet scene in *Macbeth*, and it disappears and reappears, according to Macbeth's imagination. Ghost scenes appear in *Hamlet*, and ghosts make the vision of *Richard the Third* point to the morrow.

In the New English Bible, Luke 24:39, Jesus said to his friends who were seeing him for the first time since the crucifixion, "Why are you so perturbed? Why do questionings arise in your minds? Look at my hands and feet. It is I myself. Touch me and see; no ghost has flesh and bones as you can see that I have."

Dr. Robert E. H. Peeples of Hilton Head Island says that more than once he has seen his handsome young uncle, John Williamson Peeples, Jr. (1884-1917), walking up and down the broad staircase of the big house his grandfather built in 1912 at Railroad Avenue and Fifth Street in Estill, South Carolina. Dr. Peeples says his Uncle John died eight months before he was born.

For that one in ten thousand who doesn't enjoy hearing a good ghost story, or stepping into an antebellum home where the builder makes his presence known, or peeping into a mausoleum at the empty tombs where members of a prominent planter family once were buried, or standing at the site where a lovely young girl was buried as she sat in a keg of rum, then read this book anyway. For if you take this tour, you will see these sights and more: you'll tour houses built in a long-ago age, you'll walk on riverfronts where pirates once charged ashore with their bounty, you'll visit tiny churches where the colonists worshiped, and you'll walk on cobblestone streets where the clop, clop of horses' hooves and the scraping of wagon wheels were almost dimmed by the clanging of the milk tins being banged about by dock hands.

Today these homes have been beautifully renovated, the cobblestone streets uncovered, and the riverfronts restored to resemble their swashbuckling days. Their paths are well-traveled by visitors who let their fantasies of yesteryear take over.

You'll also walk on an island wild animals still claim as their home. Alligators, wild boars, and deer still live among the pines, cedars, cypresses, live oaks and the thick growth of underbrush.

Every story in this book doesn't have a ghost, but each tale has a mysterious happening that will stir your imagination and fantasy. I have added my own flair to the tales that I felt were so scant of information and drama. This book was written for all of you: you who believe and you who don't. But don't you think it's more fun to believe?

North Carolina

About Wilmington

Wilmington, the county seat of New Hanover County, is located in the tidewater section of southeastern North Carolina. The county is bounded on the east by the Atlantic Ocean and on the west by the Cape Fear River. Major highways coming into Wilmington are U.S. 17, U.S. 421, U.S. 117, U.S. 74/76, N.C. 132 and N.C. 133.

The Cape Fear area has a rich, historic heritage. Founded 250 years ago on the Cape Fear River, Wilmington quickly developed into a thriving port city. The Old Cotton Exchange on the harbor has been graciously restored and offers visitors a leisurely opportunity to shop, dine, or just stroll through the ancient walkways and courtyards.

Since 1732 the city of Wilmington has served the lower Cape Fear region as a funnel, exporting agricultural products and importing material goods. During the Civil War, this town was the last significant Confederate port open to the daredevil blockade runners. Civil War enthusiasts enjoy artifacts and dioramas illustrating that era, including some from the Blockade Runner Museum.

Chandler's Wharf takes you back to the late nineteenth century when Wilmington's hustling and bustling wharves made her the busiest city of North Carolina. There, the Nautical Museum highlights the spirit and atmosphere of this nineteenth-century seaport. Restaurants and shops lure you inside where the charming atmosphere of days-gone-by is maintained and enhanced outdoors by cobblestone alleys, wooden sidewalks and wharves lined with barrels and rustic wagons.

Although the New Hanover County Museum, 814 Market Street, has many visitors, the atmosphere is ever so tranquil, and it is meant to be. Founded by the United Daughters of the Confederacy, this is the oldest history museum in North Carolina, and the emphasis is on what Wilmington was like during the Colonial Period.

After your visit to Wilmington, follow U.S. 421 through Carolina Beach and Kure Beach to Fort Fisher. The Fort Fisher Historic Site and Museum is the location of a large Confederate earthwork fort, the last to fall in the Civil War. Visitor Center open Tuesday through Saturday, 9 AM-5 PM, free.

The Fort Fisher Marine Resources Center has exhibits of marine life and other exhibits well worth exploring. Also, nature trails. Free.

From Fort Fisher you can travel by ferry (the ferry landing is just beyond the Fort Fisher Resources Center), to Southport, a charming coastal town. From Southport, take N.C. 211 to Supply, North Carolina, where you will connect with U.S. 17 South, traveling south to the Grand Strand.

Ferry schedules from Fort Fisher to Southport:

Summer Schedule	*Winter Schedule*
Leave Fort Fisher Landing at . . .	
8:00 AM	9:30 AM
10:00 AM	12:30 PM
12:00 Noon	2:30 PM
2:00 PM	4:30 PM
4:00 PM	
6:00 PM	

Wilmington's Haunted House
on Market Street

On any sunny morning in the office of the Wilmington Chamber of Commerce, a distinct smell of pipe tobacco pervades the air as automatic typewriters click *on*. Footsteps ascend the stairs. The sound of running water comes from the back of the building. There is nothing unusual about the scene — except for the fact that all of these movements and sounds are caused by a ghost.

"Pooh," says one of the secretaries, who has more or less kept her head about the whole thing. "You see the ghost here all the time."

It's true. The supernatural being moves like a shadow through the handsome red-brick building located at 514 Market Street, in the Historic District. Black shutters, fastened to the wall by S brackets, frame many-paned windows. The first-story rooms are high, over a tall basement, and some of the basement windows have been bricked over. A United States flag flies from the porch of this charming structure, located one and a half blocks from St. James Church. Law offices are in the vicinity.

Here you can pick up promotional information about Wilmington's famous waterfront and other attractions, but the chief scene-stealer is the ghost. Persist, and you'll hear breathless

Wilmington's Haunted House on Market Street   *Photo by Sid Rhyne*

stories about the burglar alarms that go off for no known reason; the alarm that detects movement in the room also goes off. Indeed, machines here perform all sorts of spooky feats, and the Chamber of Commerce offers the haunted house stories as an added Wilmington attraction.

The house was built in the early nineteenth century, and cabinetmakers and other artisans of that period created their best for it. Wood for bannisters, floors and mouldings came into the port on sailing vessels. Walls were built of brick that came to the harbor as ballast, and a lot of ballast went into the building of this house. The walls are 14 inches thick. Pegs, not nails, hold the long hardwood floorboards in place.

Known as the Price-Gause House, it was designed for the upper crust who appreciated the finest in prestige living. It provided everything possible to fill the special needs of the Gause family, who frequently reported the goings-on of a ghost on the premises. In their words, their house had it all, including a wandering spirit.

The ghost indicated its presence on the stairway soon after the family moved into the mansion in 1843. As they sat in the drawing room, talking over the day's activities, heavy, distinct footsteps were heard ascending the stairs. Members of the family were startled, and they rushed into the hall to see who was there.

"Listen!"

Everybody seemed to hear footsteps on the stairs. Then they stopped.

The mother tried to show more courage than the others. She stepped onto the bottom step and, in a quavering voice, asked, "Who is it? Are you there?"

But there was no answer. When she turned and saw all eyes upon her, she made an effort to act spunky. "Let's forget all about this and go back into the drawing room and talk about our new house. After all, not everyone is fortunate enough to live in a personally planned house."

One of the main pleasures for the family was having just the number and kinds of rooms they wanted, each room where they wanted it to be relative to the others and to the whole. Another kind of pleasure consisted of having the particular things they prized in this house — big brass doorknobs and the special layout of the kitchen. And then they talked about what this house was like. It was probably the most popular form of architecture for that day. Thus the rewards of having a house that was specially designed for them, ranging from what was functional to what was comfortable and convenient, was a very special pleasure. To get on, though, they talked about the possibility of this house, as new as it was, being inhabited by a spirit. And they knew not the spirit of whom. By now they were hearing footsteps somewhere overhead in the upstairs bedrooms and hallway. Could the spirit be that of the architect, or perhaps the builder? They didn't know, but they agreed that anyone who was not alarmed by the spirit in the house was an instant candidate for a head examination!

During the next 24 months that the family occupied the house on Market Street, they concluded that there was no explanation for the strange noises and no further attempts would be made to identify the ghost. He would simply be accepted as a member of the household.

The sinister movements of the ghost continued, and the house that had at first been revered was now thought of as haunted. The owners, who had formerly had such high aspirations for their beautiful home, were being pressured inexorably by the ghost whose antics touched everyone living in the structure. More and more, difficulties in the relationship of ghost and family arose.

One night as the footsteps were heard going up the stairs, a family member was stationed at the foot of the stairway to prevent the escape of the intruder. Other family members went upstairs, and they held lamps in every dark nook and cranny. But no person or thing could be found. After the search, they agreed that this time they would finally make their peace with the ghost.

As reputations go, the ghost in the house on Market Street had a good one. No one had ever seen him, and he had never brought to the family any weird accidents or misfortune. But he was tenacious and bulldogged firm; just when everyone had pulled himself together, there would be another incident. The latest one was a sound of tapping that moved along the walls, starting low and ending up just under the overhang of the roof. Later on, a servant complained that a late-night snacker was messing up the kitchen. No one in the family admitted to going into the kitchen during the night.

Guests who visited the house complained that blankets slipped from the bed and a rocking chair rocked while empty. One guest admitted having seen an inexplicable mist floating behind her as she looked into a looking glass.

In October, 1967, a reporter from the *Wilmington Star* went to the house for a story. As the reporter snooped around, composing in his mind the feature that would appear in the paper the following Sunday, unusual noises occurred. Footsteps were heard in the entrance hall, and then they ascended the steps. A photographer flew out of the drawing room and quickly snapped a photograph of the stairway. After awhile the newspaper people went back to work, and the photographer developed his film.

The finished photograph of the stairway in the house at 514 Market Street was something else again. As the photographer looked at it, he was too surprised to stir. The wood steps showed clearly, as did the graceful bannister rail of walnut. The wallpaper in the background was a colorful pattern of flowers and greenery against a white background. The image of propriety was in keeping with the story, and the picture would elicit admiration for the house from the reader. But there on the stairs was the ghost. The photographer had not seen it when he snapped the photograph, but it was in the picture nonetheless. The ghost had no discernible features, no strong nose or great profile, but it had a certain shape. Shoulders, arms and neck were clear. Although the likeness of the apparition was gauzy on the edges, the center was solid enough to blot out any print of the stairway on the other side of the ghost.

The photographer signed an affidavit verifying that he made the photograph and that it was not changed in any way to give the illusion of a ghost on the stairs. He testified that the photo had been made with a Nikon camera, and that he believed that some phenomenon was present in the house at the time he made the photograph.

The Strange Burial
of Nancy Martin

At Sea
May 25, 1857

My dear Wife,
Behold me again at sea.

With our precious daughter Nance, I shall refer to her by this our name of such affection and devotion as we have always had for our Nancy, on my one side, and our son John on my other, when I sailed from Wilmington on this voyage, I felt myself superior to depression. The present was enjoyed, and the future was anticipated with enthusiasm. But I find it my somber duty to inform you that one dreadful blow has destroyed us; reduced us to the veriest, the most sublimated wretchedness. Our Nance, on whom all rested; our daughter, our companion, our friend — she on whom we depended to transmit down the mingled blood of the union of ourselves — she who was to have redeemed all of your beauty and shed new glory upon our family — that daughter, always our content-ment and joy, is taken from us — *is dead*. I see her dead, but my hand cannot surrender her to a watery grave. By some method of preservation, I shall return our Nance to you for burial in

Wilmington, and you shall see her again before she has wasted away in death. I know not of the procedure I shall use, but I conceive it necessary to use all of my meager talents to endure whatever process I can originate to compose her body for its return to you from thousands of miles distant. If our son John were not with me, I know not what path I would take to relieve myself of this burden of seeing our Nance in death. But John is in a low state of health, and he requires unusual observation and some medical attention. I have torn myself from my own agonies to perform services for our son.

> Your devoted husband,
> Silas H. Martin

At Sea
May 27, 1857

My dear Wife,
Behold me still at sea.

I sit here again writing to you about the loss of our Nance. The letters will be posted at my next port of call, probably in Rio de Janeiro about five days hence. I expect to send my letter by someone who is going straight through, as I expect to be delayed in delivering our cargo of Carolina virgin pine lumber. It would give me great satisfaction to know that you will receive my letters before I return to you. In each port, there are ships that can be relied upon that are steered on a straight course to the Carolinas.

Of the vessels in my shipbuilding company in Wilmington, the one I chose for this voyage, the clipper, is the speediest at sail. It was my good fortune to have chosen this ship, as we are now hastening toward you, yet there seems to be nearly half a world between us.

The burial marker at the grave of Nancy Martin, affectionately called Nance by her family.   *Photo by Sid Rhyne*

Alas, in the months ahead, when we sail into the Wilmington harbor, you must not be surprised as your eyes fall on the mode of conveyance I must choose for the remains of our Nance. I am fully bent on preserving her body in order to return her to you before her burial. You will surely think the mode of mummification undignified, but when I can talk with you I shall prevail on you to understand. Now that I have perfected a plan in which I have full confidence as to the retardation of decay, my only fears are of the long journey ahead for John and me. Our sails are set and we spring to you like wildfire in the wind, protected, as always, by the Almighty.

Kindly make arrangements with the rector for Nance to be laid to rest in Oakdale Cemetery, shaded by the ancient live oak trees that are draped in moss, and brightened in the spring by dogwood blossoms.

John is low, feeble and emaciated, all over the loss of his dear sister. His complaint is an almost incessant nervous fever.

> Your devoted husband,
> Silas H. Martin

At Sea
May 31, 1857

My dear Wife,
Behold me still at sea.

I would like to see you very much. I am six thousand miles from you. I dream of you often. I am very uneasy. I fear for the suffering you will endure when we meet again.

Our Nance is now preserved for her return to you. Although I am living and faring as well as the heart could wish under the conditions, yet it is a source of great trouble to me to have to advise you of the method which I chose to transport Nance back to Wilmington. It came to me as a sort of vision, and surely, as the only election. Keep your mind in a kind and affectionate frame as you read on.

John and I took from a cabin a chair of oak and one of strength. Holding her body in a seated position, we securely tied Nance in the chair. Then we lowered the chair holding Nance, into a large cask, nailed and braced so that it is immoveable. Into the cask until Nance's head was covered, we poured many gallons of rum. The brine will impair any dehydration of the body and store the body until we reach Carolina shores. It is difficult to speak of our Nance in this way, but I expect you to depend on your faith in God as you read these words and await our return.

The ship has been rocking a good deal, and John is weak and ill with despondency over the loss of his sister and the drudgery of helping me get this vessel back home. He lies on his hammock, pondering incessantly, amid doubt, impatience and fear.

Your affectionate husband,
Silas H. Martin

Rio de Janeiro
Empire of Brazil
South America
June 2, 1857

My dear Wife,

Under the best of circumstances, traveling on the ocean is a great scenery and not attended with as much difficulty as one would imagine. But with John in his present condition, both physical and mental, disordered by solitude, pain and irritable nerves, we went into this town. Some day I shall give you a full detail of the country.

We have met with an old man from Kentucky who thinks this the finest country in the world. He says that cotton grows well, corn and wheat does well, all the fruits and vegetables thrive. The soil very rich, moderate climate with splendid water. He is going home for his family and plans to return here and buy a plantation. John and I sail tomorrow, and have no plans ever to return here. Indeed, when we sail into the Wilmington harbor, we shall ne'er leave again. I will give John a kiss for you.

No one knows of our precious cargo in the remains of our Nance, for we have told no one, and we keep the remains locked in aft cabin.

> Your affectionate husband,
> hoping this may reach you in
> health and prosperity and
> love for your husband.

At Sea
September 28, 1857

My dear Wife,
Behold me still at sea.

I write to you this morning, tho I wrote to you yesterday. I trust in the Almighty that our letters reach you, lest you lapse into terror that my silence might have been occasioned by some unfortunate accident.

Imagine yourself the feelings of a husband who has to inform you that there has indeed been an unfortunate accident on board this vessel, and we have lost our dear son John.

Last night just after the sun disappeared, a violent storm came unexpectedly from the port side. John said he would stay on deck, and I returned to my cabin. Suddenly we were being tossed about in waves the size of mountains. When the storm abated, the crew and I searched everywhere, but there was no John. His frail, sorrow-wracked body had washed overboard. John's burial at sea was by divine choice, for I would have been most careful and rigid in endeavoring to return his body to Wilmington for burial, along with his sister.

The crew assisted most astonishingly in searching the ship from prow to stern. Every available nook and cranny was visited in the hope that John would be found. But the search brought no result. I shall attend church when we put into port and pray for John's soul. I preached in an Episcopal Church on an island, and visited a Catholic Church in Rio de Janeiro. All have been very fine, but some of the strangest sermons that I ever beheld.

Adieu, my dear wife. I trust there will be no further difficulties before I reach home. God bless and preserve you.

> Your devoted husband,
> Silas H. Martin

Note: To visit the burial site of Nancy Martin, go to Oakdale Cemetery at the north end of 15th Street. Enter through iron gates between brick pillars and continue on the center road (paved) to the rear of the cemetery. Turn right just before you reach the bridges. About a block and a half (cemetery blocks are short) you will see a small white arrow that points to the Martin family burial plot, on the right. A grave marker in the likeness of two rough logs forming a cross, engraved NANCE, is among the markers at the gravesite of other family members. The Martin family plot is on a bluff, enclosed by an old fence. The tall granite stone at the resting place of Nancy Martin's parents reads:

> Silas Hosmer Martin
> Died September 4, 1861
> Aged 66 years, 1 month and 17 days.
>
> Margaret Crawford Martin
> Died January 14, 1872
> Aged 75 years, 1 month and 5 days.

Oakdale Cemetery was chartered in 1852. In this cemetery are graves of confederate leaders, officers, and soldiers, as well as many yellow fever victims.

The Martin family plot in Oakdale Cemetery in Wilmington.

Photo by Sid Rhyne

The Man
Who Was Buried Alive

"Alexander, can you hear me?" The words seeped into the room from a sort of sepulchral presence.

"Sam? Is it really you? It *can't* be you, Sam. You're dead."

"That's right, Alexander. I *am* dead. But I hadn't breathed my last breath when you and my family had me interred in Saint James churchyard last year, in eighteen hundred and ten. *I was buried alive.*"

Alexander walked to a window and turned, facing the room. His eyes searched for any trace of his deceased friend, Samuel R. Jocelyn. As his eyes explored every nook and cranny, he thought about the young man who had been his closest acquaintance. They had from time to time talked about death, and Sam once said that if he died first, he would come back and contact Alexander. Was that what he was doing now? Alexander wondered. Could it be that Sam *hadn't* expired at the time of his burial?

Alexander realized that very thing had happened before. There was no surefire way of preserving a body, although some people in science were working on a process called embalming. But now, in the early part of the nineteenth century, people were buried shortly after death, before the body began to decay. *Had they buried Sam too soon?*

Samuel R. Jocelyn was buried in this cemetery adjacent to St. James Church.   *Photo by Sid Rhyne*

Sam had come from a fine, upstanding family. His father was a counselor-at-law and respected by all of Wilmington. He would be the last person in the world to let anything so sinister happen to his beloved son.

"Alex," the voice from an unseen presence oozed, "You didn't go with me that day — the day I was found lying unconscious on the road."

"No, Sam, I didn't go with you on that day. And to tell you the truth, I've regretted it. I'd give all that I own if I had gone with you. There may have been some way I could have prevented your death."

"But, Alexander, I didn't die then. I was only unconscious."

Alexander Hostler moved like a sleepwalker to a chair and eased himself into it. "Sam, tell me what happened to you."

"I went for a ride on my stallion, Stocking Foot. Oh, the horse rode smoothly that day. With the wind in my face, we flew through the groves of oaks, and when we reached the Cape Fear River, Stocking Foot pranced to a stop. I sat there, looking beyond the river, toward the sea, thinking that I was glad to be alive. I wore my Scottish plaid kilt, the cloth being the same as that worn by the Scots of the Highlands. As you know, I've always been excited by the Scots, their thrift, their clans, their bagpipes and their tartans. The royal flag of Scotland with its red lion on a yellow background inspired me to think of red and yellow as *my* colors. Hence, my pleated skirt of red and yellow, with some blue and green, of course. I'm glad the Scots came to the Cape Fear, for they provided me with much influence and courage." The voice trailed off, then drifted back. "I got off my horse and I gazed at the river. Finally, I remounted and started home. It was when I came around the last curve, and could see the white house of two stories and the small springhouse that, uh, ..."

"And then?" Alexander urged the voice to continue with the story.

"A canebrake rattler slithered into the sandy lane. The horse's front hooves rose high, thrusting my head into the robust limbs of a tree, and I believe a limb struck me at the base of the skull, at the back of my head. It seemed that the movable parts of my body, my arms and legs, were paralyzed. I slid from the horse onto the road."

"Was it long before you were found?" Alexander asked.

"I cannot answer that question, for I lapsed into a deep coma and know nothing of what happened next. But the faint sound of voices came to me in the period of time that followed. Old Doctor Kell told my father that I had expired, and burial should take place before any decay of the body set in. I felt a sheet being pulled over my face, which I was trying with all that was within me to move away from my mouth."

"Oh, Sam. That cannot be true."

"It's quite true, Alex. If you'll go to the cemetery at Saint James and have my burial chest opened, you will see for yourself."

"Sam. I can't do that."

"But you must. It is the only way you will know the truth. And in order to prevent Dr. Kell from making this unfortunate mistake a second time, you must do it."

Alexander Hostler sat perfectly still for a moment as he contemplated what the ghost of Samuel Jocelyn had just said. Finally he responded, "Sam, I'll go to the authorities and tell them what you have told me. It will then be in their hands."

The law enforcement authorities decided to enlist the help of Dr. Kell and another physician in exhuming the body of Samuel Jocelyn. The physicians, a group of officers, a woman who represented the family of the deceased, and Alexander Hostler made up the group who were to examine the remains of Samuel Jocelyn.

As the earth was being removed, Alexander meandered

among the burial sites of other people whom he had known and who had been friends of Sam's.

Eliza Hobbs, spouse of Joel, had departed this life only two years ago. At thirty-one years, she had been in her prime, and quite beautiful. The burial site of Sarah Nutt, who had lost her life eleven years earlier, caught Alexander's eye. If he'd remembered correctly, her father was H. W. Skillings, of Boston.

Alexander stopped to examine the marker at the burial spot of Doctor Samuel Green. He hadn't really known Dr. Green, but many of his friends still talked of him. Words engraved on the stone read:

> Doctor Samuel Green
> He practiced physick and surgery
> in Wilmington thirty years with
> good success. He was a lover
> of the social virtues, a
> friend of morality. He lived in
> good esteem with mankind.

It was late in the day, and darkness was enclosing the cemetery when the casket was pulled from the ground. The physicians leaned over for a better look, and the man who called himself the magister opened the tomb. To everyone's utter surprise, the body of Samuel Jocelyn was lying face down, with his back to the top of the box. He was dressed in his Scottish kilt, and the red and yellow colors still had much clarity.

Dr. Kell went white and had to be supported by two other physicians to keep from falling to the ground.

"It's true," Alexander whispered. "Sam *was* buried alive. And he had to return from the dead in order for us to learn of the premature burial."

Note: St. James Church, of beige stucco, with a clock in the tower, faces the Cape Fear River. It sits on the corner of Third and Market streets, across from the Burgwin-Wright House where Cornwallis was headquartered. (This house is open to the public.) St. James Church cemetery is at the corner of Fourth and Market streets. Many interesting old markers can be seen, many of them cracked and embellished with lichen. St. James Parish was founded in 1729. The first church was constructed on the site in 1751, and the present church was built in 1859.

The Eradication
of the Hermit

A girl named Elizabeth (not her real name), who has tasted the thrill of seeing a ghost, visited the World War II bunker at Fort Fisher. A few years before that, she had read a book on Adolph Hitler's last days, which were spent in a bunker in Germany, and she'd become obsessed with bunkers and people who had lived in them. She had actually touched a bottle of wine said to have been taken from Hitler's underground apartment. As she moved the bottle from one position to another and watched the rich ruby liquid gurgle, she thought that Hitler had likely held this very bottle and planned to drink the claret.

Before visiting the old Fort Fisher bunker where, she had heard, a hermit had lived, Elizabeth stopped at the Fort Fisher Civil War Museum for information. She learned that the hermit had lived about 20 years in the dreary seaside fortification. A staff member at the museum told Elizabeth that in the beginning they had tried to get rid of the recluse. "We started a file labeled *The Eradication of the Hermit*," she said. "But visitors to Fort Fisher demanded that they be allowed to see him. Quite suddenly, we realized that he had become our top tourist attraction. The fact is, more people came to see the hermit than came to view the displays in the museum." After reflecting for a moment, she added, "We were unable to eradicate him, and it's a good thing. He was a natural attraction, and the receptacle where he lived draws tourists. It's an enticement for them."

"How can I find it?" Elizabeth asked.

"A trail leads from the Fort Fisher Marine Resources Center to the military building where ammunition was stored during World War II."

Elizabeth asked a woman who had seen and spoken with the hermit to accompany her to the bunker as a guide.

The path to the bunker is lined with myrtle, yaupon and huge live oak trees. Some of the oak limbs grow erratically, just over ground, then underground and back up again. Finally, they reached the building, plainly marked "Hermit Bunker."

The structure is 14 by 20 feet and made of concrete. The floor is dirt. An old mattress and springs are on the floor, and rags are scattered about. The structure is surrounded by myrtle bushes.

"How did the hermit get food?" Elizabeth wanted to know.

"He lived off the land. Netting fish, mostly. Through the years he made some friends, and they brought supplies to him."

"Was he terribly eccentric?" Elizabeth asked as she stared at the cold bunker.

"Oh sure. Anyone who lives the life of a loner is a little eccentric, I guess. But he had a sense of humor. When he was asked, 'What do people call you?', his answer was, 'I don't care what they call me so long as they call me to supper!' Honestly, there was something almost *charming* about that man."

No door hung in the opening, and Elizabeth was told that the old man stacked any lumber he could find in the doorway opening during winter months. A hole in the back wall indicated that he had perhaps had fire within the building, for cooking and keeping warm.

"Tell me something of his appearance," Elizabeth asked.

"He was a small man. Had a full beard and mustache, salt and

The Hermit leans against a boat. He has just said, "I don't care what they call me as long as they call me to supper." Ten days after this photo was made, the Hermit was dead.

The Hermit is bursting out of the bunker ready to take on the world.

Credits:
George E. Harrill, son of the Fort Fisher Hermit

Harry Warren,
Researcher at New Hanover County Museum

The Hermit's Bunker at Fort Fisher   *Photo by Sid Rhyne*

pepper, as they say. Always wore a straw hat and boots." The guide shook her head. "He was a curiosity, all right." Then she spread her hands, indicating the surrounding area. "We still believe money is buried somewhere."

"Where would a hermit get money?"

"He always placed a frying pan by the opening of the bunker," the guide explained. "Visitors dropped money into the pan. He acquired quite a sum."

"How do you know that?" Elizabeth hastened to ask.

"After his death, his family found more than a thousand dollars stashed in cans, and dollar bills had been carefully placed between the pages of old newspapers. As a matter of fact, some people believe he was murdered during an attempted robbery."

"Was he really murdered?"

"No one knows for sure. But the evidence was convincing enough that the hermit's family had his remains exhumed and examined."

"In what condition was his body found after his death?" Elizabeth asked, her eyes fixed on the bunker.

"Photos showed that the hermit's body was at the door. His plastic raincoat was bunched around his neck. Upon examination of the body, it was learned that both legs were bloody, as though they'd been dragged. And drag marks and shoe prints were also found in the sand around the door."

"Mercy, mercy," Elizabeth shuddered. "Was he sort of stand-offish to tourists who passed this way?"

"Not at all. He entertained anyone who'd listen to his philosophies. He talked about a school that he said he'd organize one day to teach people common sense."

"I wonder if he had any education to speak of," Elizabeth said, more to herself than to her companion.

"The hermit had attended college," the guide answered.

"And he also went to a school of biopsychology in Chattanooga. I believe it was the William Marcus Taylor School. For the rest of his life, he was a follower of Taylor's Unitarian philosophy."

As the women walked around the bunker, the guide said, "He did seem a little overly sensitive about his short stature, as I think back, but he loved having visitors. He even kept a register of them."

"Did the old man have any family?"

"Oh, yes. A fine family from North Carolina."

"Did they know that he lived here?"

"Yes. But I believe they, in a way, felt satisfied with the situation. The hermit was suntanned, and the staples of his diet, like seafood, kept him as healthy as possible under the circumstances."

"When did he die?"

"In June of 1972."

"Do you think he was murdered?"

The guide looked out to sea. "I don't know. It's one of the mysteries of Fort Fisher. The life of the hermit was one of the ancient syntheses of men and sea. I think that was his story: the meeting of two deep mysteries — the hermit and the sea. When two such mysteries meet, it's a lightning strike, as though the pair had been looking for years to find each other. And when they collided, they were like one sublime being, fired by the sun and the moon."

"When did he come here?"

"I don't know the answer to that one, but there's a rumor that he survived Hurricane Hazel, in October, 1954, while living here."

"Believers in ghosts think that someone who was murdered will return and cause trouble for the killer," Elizabeth whispered, not looking directly at the guide.

"Well, I don't know. It's like the waving girl, the mysterious lady who waved to passing ships day and night from her lonely home on Elba Island, near Savannah. Some people say they've seen a fluttering rag. If that's true, then it surely must be the ghost of the waving girl."

"If the ghost of the hermit returned, how do you think you would know?" Elizabeth asked.

The guide laughed. "Well, he certainly couldn't leave footprints in the sand, because ghosts don't leave footprints."

"That's for sure."

"It's a fact that he's now the best-known resident of Fort Fisher, and I think he wouldn't have it any other way, although he lived the life of a hermit. He lived his life hidden away from the eyes of outsiders, but he was friendly when they approached him. He was a kind of mystical being, and if his spirit does come back, it won't be as a melancholy oddity, but rather as a man who lived and let live."

Just then an unexpected shadow fell on Elizabeth and the guide.

Note: The hermit's son later wrote to me: "My name is George E. Harrill and I am the Hermit's son. I have expended much time, effort and money trying to solve Dad's murder. There is no doubt, as your story implies, that he was indeed murdered by the cruel and brutal method of dragging him all about the beach in a sleeping bag until he succumbed to a heart attack or some similar attack."

South Carolina

The Grand Strand

The Grand Strand is a 60-mile necklace of beaches located on a gently curving crescent of coastline, along the warm, blue Atlantic, from the North Carolina border to historic Georgetown. Some of the world's widest beaches, reaching nearly a quarter of a mile during low tides, are here. Miles and miles of clean, hard packed white sand lure sunbathers, fishermen, golfers and shell collectors to this world-famous beach area. The temperature is mild year around, warmed by the Gulf Stream 35 miles offshore. By following U.S. 17 South, you will travel this strand known as the "Seaside Golf Capital of the World."

About the turn of this century, the Grand Strand gained recognition as a resort area where one could restore oneself with the clean salt water during a morning dip. Myrtle Beach became the hub of the resort. A contest was held in 1900 to choose a name for the village, and Adeline Cooper Burroughs submitted the winning name *Myrtle Beach*. A new lifestyle developed with the coming of the golfers during the 1960s, and during the 1970s, entrepreneurs built condominiums facing golf course greens and fairways as well as the ocean. The 1980s brought an inpour of tour buses, and only the imagination can take a stand on what the 1990s will bring to this strand.

Alice Flagg

It is a common story, the tale of Alice Flagg, but as one hears more details of this sad narrative, it becomes dazzling. For Alice Flagg is the most popular ghost on South Carolina's famed Grand Strand. The Alice Flagg story began in 1849 when she lived with her brother, Dr. Allard Flagg, and their mother in Murrells Inlet. They lived at The Hermitage, which was the seashore home of the owners of Wachesaw Plantation during the colonial period. This is a case of the mother and brother becoming deeply involved in the life of a young girl when she fell in love with a man believed to be beneath her station in South Carolina aristocracy.

"Every woman must leave her mark on the earth," Alice's mother whispered to her. "And how can you etch on this earth anything that's worthwhile if you attach yourself to this common lumberman?"

But Alice was obsessed with her young man and paid scarce attention to her mother and her brother. However, one day when the tall, clean-cut lumberman came to call and Alice was about to step into the carriage with him, her brother stormed out of The Hermitage, and yelled, "Wait!"

He refused to allow Alice to ride with her young man, and he forced the lumberman to ride a horse while he, Dr. Flagg, sat in the carriage beside Alice. Alice felt she was suffering under the

THE HERMITAGE: The house in Murrells Inlet where Alice
Flagg died.   *Photo by Sid Rhyne*

tyranny of her family, and she hotly resented their unrestrained exercise of power. She was wretched, and for all she could tell, her mother and brother didn't care!

While her mother and brother had extolled the virtues of falling in love with someone who would be a glorious addition to the Flagg family, Alice could not relate to their arguments, spoken with great fervor. She accepted an engagement ring from her true love. Dr. Allard Flagg staunchly refused to allow Alice to wear the ring on her finger, so she attached it to a ribbon and concealed it around her neck. As the days passed, she believed she was successful in concealing the ring. But one day her mother discovered the ring on her chest and another fighting match flared. The mother shouted that the lumberman was deplorable and plebeian and unfashionable as well — worthy of no better wife than a common shop girl!

After suffering undue abuse, Alice was unable to persuade her mother and her brother to change their attitudes toward her betrothed, and under their bitter arguments she agreed to leave Murrells Inlet for Charleston where she would attend school.

But living in Charleston, with the change of terrain and the sensation of being alone in the pastel port city — plus what seemed to be a lifetime of grief over her lost love — took its toll on Alice. She became frail and listless and complained of some discomfort in the left side of her head. Lying on her bed, crying into her pillow, she carved in her mind a track of her life without the man she loved, and the track ended, always, in a blur, an indistinct ending to her future. When she had first arrived in Charleston, she had been able to look with stark clarity on her predicament, but now it was blinding, a remarkable silence that she couldn't comprehend. Was she to survive this, she wondered.

One night, as she lay on her bed, although she was in a southern port city, she began to think that she was trying to walk in deep snow. It was a mystical experience as she pulled herself through deep white powder, struggling, and then, floating. The wilderness was on a grand scale of sky-high white spires, ancient glaciers and faraway valleys. Later that night, word went from the school that Alice had taken sick and should be sent to her home in Murrells Inlet.

When her brother received the word, he left at once in his carriage, but the way was long and arduous. Four days later he reached Charleston. He found Alice incredibly fatigued, with no strength to even nod to him. Her stamina had evaporated, and her nerves seemed in knots. He carried her to his carriage, and one of her friends packed her favorite dress for the journey. It was another four-day trip back home. The jostling and jolting as the carriage convulsed and bumped on the uneven roadway and across several rivers by ferry heightened Alice's nervousness. When she reached home, she was substantially weakened and soon lapsed into a coma and died.

Alice Flagg was dressed in her favorite dress for her funeral at All Saints Church, but her engagement ring had been taken away. Her corpse wasn't one of beauty. Her waxy face clearly showed the pain of losing her true love, and then, her life.

A plain marble slab, engraved ALICE, was placed over her burial mound.

Myriad friends and relatives say they have seen Alice's apparition at her home, The Hermitage at Murrells Inlet, and in the burial ground at All Saints Waccamaw Episcopal churchyard. It is believed that she comes back to search for her lost engagement ring.

When a group of young people stood at the gravesite of Alice Flagg, a ring suddenly flew off the finger of one of the girls. It took the group much of the day to locate the ring, which was treasured. The girl had been unable to remove the ring from her finger for several years due to a weight gain.

Note: Clarke A. Willcox, owner of The Hermitage in Murrells Inlet, opens his home each week for visitors to see the home of Alice Flagg. Some people question whether Alice Flagg was buried in All Saints Church cemetery. The gate at All Saints Church is usually open, and you can walk among the grave markers of the rice planters, the people who lost their lives during the terrible hurricane of Oct. 13, 1893, and see the gravesite marked *ALICE.* All Saints Church is on S.C. 255, about three miles west of Pawleys Island.

This plain marker with only one word, ALICE, discloses the place where Alice Flagg was laid to rest. *Photo by Sid Rhyne*

The Curse of the Wachesaw Skulls

Are skulls imbued with the power
of the deceased persons? Can they
emit serenity and devotion, or
radiate sardonic influence or disease?

Edwin O. Fulton stood in his workshop on the grounds of Wachesaw Plantation at Murrells Inlet and fondled a piece of wood. About the room were tables, benches and other pieces of furniture fashioned by this master craftsman. Dozens of preserved deer heads with sharp-tipped antlers were attached to overhead beams. This man, as skillful a hunter as a cabinetmaker, had taken the deer in his many hunts on the plantation.

Fulton ran his hand along a piece of wood to determine the kind of product the well-seasoned, knotted wood would make. Then he held it to a window and viewed a distortion in the grain. His head nodded satisfaction as he decided the deformity of the cypress would enhance the characteristic of the table he planned.

"What's up?" the cabinetmaker asked, as he tipped a table and let a mound of sawdust fall to the floor.

"I want to know about the skulls," the visitor asked. "The Indian skulls that you found here on Wachesaw Plantation.

"You an Indian relic fan?" Fulton asked.

"No. Just interested in the skulls. I've heard they carry a kind of, uh, wish that misfortune, or evil, befall another."

"Let's go over to the house," Fulton said as he reached for a cane. The arthritis in his back was a nuisance. In the living room of the comfortable, cozy home, Edwin Fulton spoke of the Wachesaw skulls.

The Wachesaw excavation site was first uncovered in the late 1920s when a man named Chandler worked with Fulton on a cabin being built as a hunting lodge for the couple who had purchased the plantation. This was during the time that the old families were selling their Low Country plantations to people from the North who used the old rice fields as places to hunt ducks. Wachesaw had been one of the most historic and beautiful of the South Carolina rice plantations.

During the nineteenth century when rice was at its peak of production, Wachesaw Plantation was the northernmost plantation in the Georgetown district, on the eastern side of the Waccamaw River. The master of Wachesaw Plantation was Dr. Allard Belin (pronounced Blane) Flagg, brother of Alice Flagg. Wachesaw came to Dr. Flagg as a gift from an uncle, the Reverend James L. Belin. Dr. Flagg married Penelope Bentley Ward on Jan. 16, 1850. She was the eldest daughter of Joshua John Ward of Brookgreen Plantation, the richest rice planter of that day. At that time, the planters of the Waccamaw region set themselves into a small group, above the rest of society. But first had come the Indians to this land.

The Indians that occupied this region were of the Eastern Siouan tribes, and they included the Winyahs and the Waccamaws. The Waccamaws are believed to have had four villages populated by 210 males and 400 females in the early eighteenth century. They established a trading post near Wachesaw in 1716. The Waccamaws were destroyed in

Indian trading beads in The Charleston Museum

Courtesy of The Charleston Museum, Charleston, S.C.

1720 after 60 of their 100 braves made war on the settlers and were captured and sent to the West Indies to be sold into slavery.

While Chandler and Fulton worked on the construction of the hunting lodge at Wachesaw Plantation, Chandler lived in a house on the plantation near the site of construction. Fulton also lived on Wachesaw Plantation, and he and his wife live in the same house today.

One day as Fulton and Chandler were digging, they came upon something that seemed so unusual they took great care so as not to break the object. Cautiously, they removed dirt, sometimes using a shovel, other times using their hands. As they stripped away the earth, Fulton gasped at what he saw emerging. A skeleton! Then, as more earth was dug away, another skeleton was visible. Then three. After they had finish-ed removing the dirt, seven Indian skeletons were spread before them, each in a crouched position, with the knees drawn up under the chins. Despite Fulton's instinctive repulsion, he was surprisingly observant. The eye sockets had been stuffed with Indian trading beads. But more than any other part of the skulls, the teeth caught his attention. "They were the largest front teeth I've ever seen. Some of them had been worn down, and there were only stubs left near the gums. But others had front teeth as large as my thumb."

It appeared to Fulton, and to Chandler as well, he said, that the skulls were unusually small and remarkably well preserved, despite a yellow tinge hinting of age. And like all skulls, these had the classic mockery of mirth. They were grinning!

Word of the discovery was dispatched to the Charleston Museum, and men from Charleston arrived on the scene and removed the skeletons. The remains from the Wachesaw ex-cavation were examined by experts, who made estimates of the sex and age of the individuals. Although not enough material was found to age the Indian remains accurately, they appeared to range in age from 20 to 45 years.

Not long after the skeletons were found, Fulton was plowing the banks of an old road near the now-completed hunting lodge. The roadway had become gutted, making travel impossible. While Fulton was repairing the road, he found what he thought were two clay urns. As he examined them, out fell the remains of two Indian infants. The tiny skulls were stuffed with Indian trading beads, which, it was later learned, consisted of eleven distinct types that dated from 1600. (The urns and infant remains were sent to the Charleston Museum.) The baby skulls were delicately formed, when compared with the skulls Chandler and Fulton had discovered earlier. But the baby faces, like the adult ones, were smiling.

Under what circumstances had the children died, Fulton wondered. As he talked about it to others who came to view the tiny heads, it was assumed that the children had probably died of some disease that had swept·through the Indian village once located on the banks of the Waccamaw River, where Wachesaw Plantation now stands. For that matter, the adult skeletons could have been the remains of some people who had died from a dreaded disease on the rampage. That seemed to be a logical explanation for the mass Indian burial.

Other questions arose. If bacteria had been present at the time of the burial, could it be lying dormant in the skulls?

"You know," Fulton said, leaning back in his rocking chair, interlacing his fingers across his forehead, "strange things occurred after we found the skulls. Chandler, who worked on construction of the hunting lodge and helped me examine the skulls, had a child who came down with diphtheria. And then my son, Edwin O. Fulton, Jr., came down with diphtheria. I asked Dr. Norris, who owned Litchfield Plantation at that time, about it. Dr. Norris said it was entirely possible that the bacteria that causes diphtheria, *Corynebacterium diphtheriae*, was still active in the skulls of the Indians who were buried at Wachesaw."

Naturally, this heightened the interest in the Indian skulls. Were they invoking evil on those who found them? A curse? The people of Wachesaw began to have dreams that were so real they seemed to be visions. In the visions, there was always an Indian warrior, an unusually large man with big teeth, standing nearby. Along with the visions came eerie sounds and flashes of lightning. Then someone reported seeing several Indians fighting one another over the relics that had been unearthed at Wachesaw. A flash of lightning suddenly took the Indian braves away. Laborers who worked at Wachesaw also reported strange sights, like Indians disappearing into snow clouds.

Today a new Wachesaw Plantation is emerging. Wachesaw Plantation Limited Partnership purchased the plantation several years ago for $3.2 million. The developers' construction project calls for 733 residential units, single-family lots, duplex cottages, villas, great houses, a golf course and marina. The partnership is also financing diggings conducted by archaeologists contracted through the University of South Carolina. Already uncovered from the acidic soil at Wachesaw are three human remains from the Mississipian Period and one from the protohistoric period, a period when the Indians had contact with the Europeans.

Wachesaw Plantation is being developed into a private eighteenth century resort plantation. Huge yellow dirt carriers are moving earth for a golf course, and roads are being built. By the time this book is published, new residents will be living on the plantation. Should they be warned that Indian skulls are at rest under the moss-draped oaks by the Waccamaw River? And they are not impassive. They are grinning!

Note: To reach Wachesaw Plantation, turn onto Wachesaw Road from U.S. 17 in Murrells Inlet and drive two miles to the Waccamaw River. Wachesaw Plantation is near the Wacca Wache Marina, by the river.

Theodosia Burr

The Waccamaw Neck was a lonely place for the 17-year-old bride. Her father, Aaron Burr, hadn't encouraged Theodosia's marriage to Joseph Alston of South Carolina. But Joseph, who had finished college before he was 17 years old and had finished the training for the practice of law, had convinced Theo that he was a man of considerable courage, refinement and training; he would some day bring notice to himself. Although Theo was not in love with Joseph, and her friends discouraged her move to the swamps of the Waccamaw region of South Carolina, she gave him her hand in marriage.

The coast of South Carolina was like a foreign country to her. Girls there didn't walk hours on end while balancing books on their heads in order to learn to walk as straight as a rod. Nor did they bury their heads in language books in order to speak fluent French and other tongues. Instead, they wore frilly dresses, fretted over who swung down the Virginia reel line with whom, and never went out without at least two body servants accompanying them. It was so wasteless, so desolate. It all made Theo sick. *Really* sick. She took to her bed more and more in order to blot out the useless goings-on in the mosquito-infested, God-forsaken land in which she had chosen to live with her new husband.

Ocean where Theodosia Burr is sometimes seen suspended above the water   *Photo by Sid Rhyne*

Joseph did everything in his power to make Theo comfortable and happy. He encouraged her to continue the studies of the subjects she enjoyed, inspired her to write long accounts of her new life to her father, and consoled her when she was pale and her strength waned. And he never failed to remind her that for one so young, he had inherited an extraordinary plantation from his grandfather. The grandfather's name was also Allston, but he spelled it with two ls.

Joseph Allston's will provided:

> July 1784
> I Give and Devise to my Grandson
> Joseph Allston (son of William Allston)
> when he arrives to ye age of Twenty four
> years old that plantation or Tract of Land
> Will'd to me by my Father with all ye
> Island of Swamp Lands over against ye same.
> Also one other Tract of Land joining ye
> same which I purchased of my brother John
> Allston makeing in the whole about One
> Thousand Three Hundred acres more or less.

The plantation was named The Oaks, and a new house was constructed there for Joseph and Theodosia after their marriage in 1801. But as far as Theo was concerned, all of the plantation was an "island of swamp lands." The mosquitoes brought blood when they punctured your skin.

Theo's health further deteriorated with each year and her only happiness came as she wrote long letters to her father and doted on her only child, a boy named Aaron Burr Alston.

When Theo's father challenged Alexander Hamilton to a duel, he didn't know if he would survive the contest, and he wrote Theo a heart-tearing letter:

Georgetown building in which Theodosia Burr Alston waited
for her sailing vessel to leave   *Photo by Sid Rhyne*

I am indebted to you, my dearest
Theodosia, for a very great portion
of the happiness which I have enjoyed
in this life. You have completely
satisfied all that my heart and
affections had hoped or even wished.
With a little more perseverance,
determination, and industry, you will
obtain all that my ambition or vanity
had fondly imagined. Let your son have
occasion to be proud that he had a mother.
Adieu.   Adieu.

The day after this letter was written, Burr and Alexander Hamilton met on a grassy, wooded knoll in Weehawken Heights, New Jersey. It was July 11, 1804. The men refused last-minute reconciliation. They walked off ten paces. Each took his position. They turned and fired. Hamilton fell, mortally wounded.

Burr fled to Pennsylvania and again wrote to his daughter, but Theo could not be consoled. Why had life failed her, she wondered. Nothing could be straightened out.

In the years that followed, Theo's health went from bad to worse, in mind as well as body. She spent most of her time lying on a long cushioned seat, without back or arms, and placed against a wall. Her body servants waited on her constantly, holding damp cloths to her forehead, and speaking soothing words. On Jan. 11, 1811, she wrote to her father:

Imagine yourself the feelings of a
woman whose naturally irritable nerves
were disordered by severe illness, and
who, during weeks of solitude, and pain,

and inoccupation, lay pondering incessantly,
amid doubt and impatience, and hope and
fear, on the subject which mingled
through the whole extent of her soul.

Eighteen months later, when the weather was humid, the Alstons left for a holiday at their cottage at the seashore. While there, Theo's son took a head cold. Joseph sent for several physicians but they were unable to save his life. He died on June 30, 1812.

Both Theo's husband and father insisted that she visit her father who was now back in New York. A friend wrote to Theo's father saying that Theo was bent on making the trip, as she was low, feeble and emaciated. Her complaint was an almost incessant nervous fever.

She set sail from Georgetown on *The Patriot* on Dec. 30, 1812. *The Patriot*, after it disappeared over the horizon, was never heard from again.

On foggy nights, if you stand on the beach at Huntington Beach State Park, you may see the slender figure of Theodosia Burr Alston suspended above the water. With her declining health after her marriage and the birth of her son, and the death of her cherished son, it is no wonder that the spirit of Theodosia comes back to the sea near her home.

Note: The Oaks Plantation is a part of Brookgreen Gardens.

Doctor Flagg

Dr. J. Ward Flagg spent his last years in his cottage at what is today Brookgreen Gardens, recounting the terrible storm that struck on Oct. 13, 1893, and washed his family to sea. Although many encouraged Dr. Flagg to walk outside in the sunlight and to attend the sick people at Brookgreen Plantation, for several years after the tragedy, he rarely left his house except for an occasional walk on the sand at the tideline. While he strolled there, he said, the dear ones who lost their lives in the storm returned and walked with him. In 1938 Dr. Flagg died. He and the other members of his family sometimes return to the scene of one of the most violent storms ever to crash on the beach that is known today as Huntington Beach State Park.

In October, 1893, the Flagg family of Brookgreen went to their cottages on the seashore portion of their property. Dr. Flagg and his parents stayed in one cottage; his brother and his wife and five of their six children were in the house next door. In those days, that beach was called Magnolia Island.

On October 12, a breeze became a boisterous wind and rain saturated the atmosphere. A man who remained on the plantation, Reverend Cato, gave an eyewitness account of the storm:

Dr. J. Ward Flagg, who survived the storm of October 13, 1893, chats with Archer Milton Huntington who, with his wife Anna, created Brookgreen Gardens.

Photo Courtesy Brookgreen Gardens

The tide ain't run out that day. Not even for to
show the oysters on the rock, nor the sand bar.
Water rushing in. Over on the beach, the sea
been light up. Been light up like lantern lights
up the house. Looked same like fire. That sea
make us think of judgment and hell. Sea
looked like it on fire. And the creek been light
up. And the tide. She rolled in fast. The moss
was flying from trees same like bird. Every
which-er-way, the trees snap. Rotten limbs fall
all round. The sound of prayers reached us.
They was all praying. Good and bad was
united. We go down in prayer. Speak to the
Good God. Ask Him to calm the elements. Beg
him to say, 'Peace Be still.'

After the wind calmed and the sea turned back, the sun came
out. All was quiet. Devastation was everywhere. Dr. J. Ward
Flagg had saved himself by hanging onto the limbs of a beach
cedar tree. He gripped the tree with such force that when
rescuers reached him, each finger had to be prized up, one by
one. His father and mother had been swept from the tree into a
wave estimated to be 40 feet high. Dr. Flagg's brother, his wife
and five children lost their lives. The beach was in wreck and
ruin.

A dead woman's shoes were unbuttoned down to the last
button. Another woman's body was found rolled up in a roll of
wire. Animals, furniture and clothing hung in trees. A tiny coat
and stocking hung on a bush.

Search parties quickly formed to locate the dead. The remains
of those who had lost their lives were sent to area churches for
burial. For several days the rector of All Saints Church near
Pawleys Island remained at the church to conduct funerals as
wagons bearing bodies rolled into the churchyard.

Dr. Flagg, overcome with grief over his lost family, went to his cottage at Brookgreen and refused to come outside. Tom Duncan, who had lost his mother and a son in the storm, took care of Dr. Flagg. Duncan cooked for him and cleaned the house. He also urged his friend to leave the house, but the physician refused. A friend named Ben Horry spoke of that time: "After they all bury and gone and Doctor stay in his house and don't come out, and I tell you God's truth, that right when the Doctor turn to he toddy. The whiskey keg what he buy would full this place up to the top!"

Finally, Dr. Flagg left his house and walked on the beach where he collected articles that washed in on the tide. Until the day he died, some of the artifacts he found at the water's edge hung on the walls of his house. He said that while he walked the beach, he talked with his father and mother and other members of his family. He believed they came back to him only as he walked on that beach, the scene of the tragic storm. If you walk the tideline of this beach, you can perhaps hear the faint cries and see the misty forms of members of the Flagg family as they recount the horror of that Friday, Oct. 13, 1893.

Note: Huntington Beach State Park is opposite U.S. 17 from Brookgreen Gardens, south of Murrells Inlet.

The Ghost
of the Crab Boy

Bryan came to the marsh (he called it the creek) at what is to-day Huntington Beach State Park to catch stone crabs for his family and for friends like Miss Addie McIntyre. Stewed crab was a staple in his diet, and he believed crabmeat had a restorative effect for one who was ill.

"The house we stay in be a two room house with one of these end chimneys, and it be over there cross the King's Road on Miss Addie McIntyre place. She been sick in bed for four weeks, but she mendin some now. She been mighty low. She feed on crabs what I bring her from the creek, and sometimes it help a little bit, but not too much."

There are about a thousand different kinds of crabs, but the stone crab is noted as the best tasting of the crabs that are consumed. It is a crustacean and lives within a hard shell. The body is broad and more or less flattened, and the five pairs of walking legs are jointed. As if that were not enough, the stone crab has snapping claws that are exceptionally strong. This story of Bryan is justifiable proof of the power of the claws of a stone crab.

Stone crabs live in holes which they hollow in the marsh mud. Those who look for these crabs can immediately identify

Low tide at the marsh where the crab boy lost his life.

Photo by Sid Rhyne

their holes. As they burrow into the mud on the bank of the marsh when the tide is low, they throw up behind them seashells and debris that had been deposited there by rising tides. Each stone crab's hole is encircled in a mixture of shells and mud.

Bryan could spot a stone crab's hole quicker than a bullet could hit its mark. I mean, he'd just reach right down into the hole and pull out the crab, and he acquired a surefire technique of getting the crab without the crab snapping his fingers.

"The crab holes," he once explained, "been same long as my arm. I worked my hand down the hole slow, and when I feel like I be gettin near the crab, I dig my fingers down in the mud. Then I yank out a passel of mud, and the crab be in that mud. I always go in the hole that way, and get what I want. It not be too much trouble. Most people use a long wire, with a hook on the end, but that be a pack of foolishness. I just reach in and get 'em."

After filling his bucket, Bryan would go home and pick the meat out of the body and claws. His mother really knew how to stew crabs. She'd put the crabmeat into the stewpot and add a little pepper and salt and a mite of nutmeg. Then she'd add the yolks of two broken up eggs, some crumbled-up biscuit and a spoonful of vinegar. While the crabs were stewing, she'd make a pan of fresh biscuits that were just right for sopping. Man, when you sopped those biscuits in the stewed crabs, now that was real eating!

One evening Bryan came to the marsh and extended his arm into a crab hole. It was getting late, and he didn't use his usual precaution in taking the crab. Suddenly, the claws of the crab clamped down on Bryan's middle finger and nearbout cut it off. But the crab held on. Bryan let out a hollar that was heard nearly to his home across the King's Road. He flailed around in the air, jumping, screaming, yelling, but the crab would not let go.

The old crab just clamped his claws tighter. Bryan, his whole arm down in the hole, pictured the crab, his eyes on their short stalks, looking amused at *his* catch.

After awhile, Bryan got tired and he couldn't scream quite so loudly. His yells became more of a mournful wail than a shrill cry, and his face lay on the marsh mud. By this time it was getting late, really late, and although Bryan told himself that there was nothing to worry about, he knew in his heart of hearts it would take a world of luck to save him. The tide would be coming in soon, and unless the crab turned him loose, the tide would rise over his body. When the tide went back out, he'd be nothing more than a limp corpse. Or maybe a stiff one. He didn't know which.

Bryan continued to wail, but no person heard him. A creeping chill began to possess him, and he peered over the marsh to the trees. He could see a lamp in a cottage in the trees. Everything was quiet, except for the incoming surf. Even the dogs were quiet. Not one howled. It came to Bryan's mind that no one was going to save him. And the crab never once lightened its grip on the boy's finger.

A grim sense of blackness, and the hopelessness of fate, seized the soul of the weary boy gripped in the tongs of the crab's claws. Bryan had gotten himself into trouble, and there was downright nothing he could do in self-defense. What have I done? he asked himself. How did I get into this mess? His voice was little more than a squeak, small and thin, but still human. "Help me. For God's sake, help me." As the tide came closer, he thought that if the rising water took his life, God would take him to the land of Canaan where he and Joshua were having a happy time.

The tide came in, then went back out. Daylight came. That was when the body of Bryan was found. He was taken to Heaven's Gate Church, and a funeral was held. Bryan was buried at the edge of the marsh, where high-tide waters would cover his grave, since the family superstition ruled that the sea must again receive its own dead or it would claim a new victim.

One night after all the chores were done around the seaside homes, a thunderstorm rolled in. Black clouds skudded just overhead and rolling thunder shook the earth. Moss hanging from the live oaks blew every which way, and rain came in sheets. In all of this, a voice was heard. "Help me. For God's sake, help me." It was believed to be the voice of Bryan.

If you walk the beach at Huntington Beach State Park, and dark clouds come in from the sea, and the color of the ocean changes from blue to gray, and the surface of the water turns choppy, and the soft warm air turns chill, listen. You may hear the voice of Bryan. It's during the storms on that beach that he comes back, still begging someone to release him from the claws of the stone crab.

A Bride, A Groom
and A Church Full of Ghosts
(As If Told by Natalie Tucker)

It was in the summer of 1918. I was invited to Pawleys Island
to attend a house party, and in those days no bridge linked
Georgetown, where I lived, and the Waccamaw Neck. The last
ferry for that night had left the Front Street Dock, so my
friends, Bootsie and Charles, and I boarded a gasoline launch,
which we hired to take us to the landing at Hagley Plantation,
the nearest point to Pawleys Island. My boyfriend, Eugene, was
to meet us at Hagley Landing.

Just as the launch reached the Hagley dock, I could see
Eugene in profile, in the moonlight. He was lying on the wharf,
and if I didn't miss my guess, he was sound asleep. It wasn't at
all like Eugene to lapse into a deep sleep while waiting for us.
Although he had met us at Hagley before, as he was the only
one of us who owned an automobile in those days, to my
knowledge he'd never stretched out on the dock and napped.

The launch idled up to the wood dock, and Eugene jerked
awake and rubbed his eyes. As I stepped to the dock, I could
see him clearly, and he looked as though he'd seen a ghost.
What I didn't know then was that he'd seen not only one
ghost, but a bride and groom, and a church full of spirits.

"Eugene, are you ill?" I asked.

"No. At least I don't think so," he answered, shaking his head as though to clear it of cobwebs.

"Well, you look faint," I persisted. "Don't you think we'd better sit down for a rest before we go to Pawleys?"

"Hush!" he snapped. "Don't let Bootsie and Charles hear."

Eugene helped Bootsie and Charles into the back seat of his car, and then he helped me into the passenger seat where I would sit next to him. He cranked the car, and when he got inside, I again thought that he looked a little pale and shaken. He didn't say anything, and in order to pass the time I began to talk about Hagley Plantation. It was a regular pastime of mine, talking of Hagley, for my ancestors, the Tuckers of Litchfield, had been very fond of the Westons of Hagley. This plantation was a lonely place in 1918, remote and overgrown, but during the nineteenth century it had been one of the liveliest plantations in the South.

Hagley furniture had been handcrafted in Charleston and England, and silver teapots and coffee urns also came from England. Heavy damask draperies hung at the ceiling-to-floor windows. But Hagley was especially famous for the food. The owner of Hagley had a rather rigid conception of prosperity. One of the principles that governed his plantation, in order for the master to appear prosperous, was to always be prepared to serve a large number of guests with no advance notice. And not only that, but to offer more food than could possibly be consumed. As I think back on it now, the most celebrated example of this was during the Civil War when the master of Hagley, Plowden Weston, invited all of the men of Confederate Company A of the Tenth South Carolina Rifle Guards to Hagley for a meal. Weston sent word to the servants that 150 men would be dining at Hagley that day. Servants at the plantation consisted of Hector, head servant; Prince, coachman; Caesar, Jack and

Gabriel, footmen; Rachel, washerwoman; Josephine and Dolly, seamstresses; Phyllis and Susanna, cooks; and Mary, the housemaid. There were many others, as well.

The company of men arrived at Hagley within three hours of the time that Weston had issued the invitation. The entire company was seated at tables set up in Weston's dining room and drawing room. The men dined on turkey, duck, rice, vegetables, pastries, bread and wines. The tattered men consumed a feast that was fit for royalty.

Eugene hadn't responded to my talk of Hagley, but I went right on with my dissertation. Just in case he didn't remember much of what I'd told him of the Hagley library, I would tell him again about the collection of expertly bound books that were valued, even in that day, at fifty thousand dollars. The volumes included Shakespeare, Moliere, Sir Thomas Browne, Arabian Nights (in French), Pascal's letters, and whole sets of sermons, prayers and folk songs. But nothing about the manor house quite compared in beauty with the chapel at Hagley. Its symmetry was magical. In 1858 Plowden and Emily Weston relocated their slave village and had St. Mary's Chapel erected on a bluff that overlooked the Waccamaw River. Pews were carved of oak, and the receptacle for water used in baptisms was of English granite. There were high, narrow, stained-glass windows, a clock and a bell.

All the while that I went on about the mystical qualities of the plantation during the last century, Bootsie and Charles were talking quietly in the back seat. Just then, as Eugene drove around a curve in the sandy roadway, three people stepped from behind a huge oak tree. They stood directly in front of the car. Eugene had to apply the brakes and send the automobile into a slide in order to avoid hitting them. The car choked to a stop, and I noticed that the girl was wearing a bridal gown, one young man was attired in the clothing of a groom, and the other young man wore the uniform of a Confederate soldier.

"Eugene!" Charles called out. "What in the name of the devil do you think you're doing?"

By this time the three people who'd appeared in the road had vanished, even more quickly than they'd appeared.

"Eugene, I believe you're trying to toss me into Charles's lap," Bootsie teased.

"Yes," Eugene said solemnly. "That's just what I did, too."

Eugene had to get out of the car and crank it to get it going again. There was no mention of the incident until we arrived at the beach house at Pawleys Island. Bootsie and Charles jumped out of the car and ran inside to join the other guests.

"Wait here minute, Natalie," Eugene said, taking one of my hands in his.

"Eugene," I murmured, "I know why you stopped the car so quickly."

"You do?"

"There were three people in the road. I saw them."

"You did?" He was alarmed, and that was plain to see.

"Was there a . . . what were they like?"

"There was a bride and a groom, and a Confederate soldier."

"Natalie," he said, "you may think that I've partaken of the strong and heady Carolina beer when I tell you what I'm going to say, but I've had not a drop."

"Tell me, Eugene, what is it you are trying to say?"

And then Eugene told me this story, and this is exactly what he said:

As I sat on the dock, waiting for the launch from Georgetown to arrive, I dozed off and a vision came to me that I shall remember the rest of my days. I was standing with a crowd of people in front of the Hagley plantation chapel. A wedding was in progress within the church, and a few people had gathered on the outside of the chapel, waiting for the wedding party to

Eugene hit the brake to avoid hitting the ghosts that appeared in front of his car on this road.   *Photo by Sid Rhyne*

come from the church. In a few minutes the bridal party came out, and all of the guests followed them. They, as well as the people on the outside, were dressed in clothing that was fashionable in the 1860s. Guests crowded around the bride and groom, prescribing formulas for future happiness. Just then a soldier in a Confederate uniform rode up on a horse that obviously had been pushed beyond its endurance. The horse's head hung nearly to its knees, and foam dropped from the nag's mouth. The soldier dismounted and confronted the bride. She threw her hands over her face and sobbed, "It's too late. I've just married another." The soldier pointed to the groom and shouted, "You married him?" "I waited for three years," the bride cried. "I thought you'd been killed in battle." The soldier turned to the groom and said, "You need not have cause for concern. You will never see me again. It is the only thing to do." Then the soldier ran to the dock and jumped into the water which was flowing downstream, out to sea with the tide. As everyone watched the soldier disappear in the dark water, the bride threw herself into the Waccamaw River at just the same spot where her former beau had disappeared. And then the groom followed his bride into the murky water. And, Natalie, at that very moment, all the people who had attended the wedding disappeared as though in a vapor.

I asked Eugene if the bride and groom and the soldier were the ones we had seen on the Hagley road.

"The very ones," he answered.

Note: Hagley Plantation today is a residential community, Hagley Estates, located opposite U.S. 17 from the South Entrance to Pawleys Island. Fairways and greens of Seagull Golf Club thread through the property, but remnants of the old plantation remain. Huge oak trees are hundreds of years old, and abandoned rice fields by the river are traces of the prosperous rice plantation. Perhaps the ghosts of the bride and groom and soldier can be seen on Hagley Boulevard on dark and misty nights.

The plantation chapel was dismantled after the Civil War. Hardware and oak stalls were given to Prince Frederick Pee Dee Episcopal Church (no longer in existence), and the beautiful stained glass windows were given to Prince George Winyah Episcopal Church in Georgetown, at the corner of Church and Broad streets. This historic church dates from the mid-1700s, and was occupied by British soldiers during the Revolution. It is open to visitors.

Pawley's Island today has many reminders of the summer of 1918. Some of the old island houses are still in existence, but there are excellent shopping facilities on U.S. 17, such as the famous Hammock shop, where Pawley's Island hammocks are made.

The Hagley Landing stood here.

Photo by Sid Rhyne

Georgetown

Georgetown, on U.S. 17 at the southernmost point of the Grand Strand, where the Waccamaw, Black, Pee Dee and Sampit rivers meet and form Winyah Bay, is rich in history and steeped in tradition. The people who live in Georgetown today still eat a bowl of rice every day and revere their ancestors. Times change. People change. But in Georgetown the duty to the heritage of the old families flourishes. The City of Georgetown Historic District is on the National Register of Historic Places.

Georgetown houses are on lots measuring 100 x 217.9 feet as laid out by William Swinton in 1734. Townhouses of the planters are evident on streets with names like Screven, Highmarket, Queen, Broad, King, Prince and Front. The South Carolina Ports Authority constructed a single-berth facility of a 500-foot dock and 60,000-square-foot transit shed. Both of these are run in order to stimulate ocean transportation in and out of Georgetown.

Plantation owners still come into this town to attend services at Prince George Winyah Episcopal Church. Perhaps their attitude is best illustrated by a remark by the owner of Wicklow Hall Plantation. "We don't own the boxed-in pews like the rice planters did, but we arrive at church thirty minutes early in order to sit in our usual pews."

The Headless Sentry

It would be a hundred years before the War Between the States would be fought on this ground, but during the American Revolution a little civil war was being staged in the South Carolina Low Country. Especially within the walls of the magnificent plantation manor houses by the four great rivers that merged at Winyah Bay in Georgetown, the Sampit, the Black, the Pee Dee, and the Waccamaw rivers. During this war between Great Britain and her American colonies, some were well disposed to the crown, while others fought with fervor to attain their independence and hold eastern South Carolina from the British. At Wedgefield Plantation, near Georgetown, a difference of loyalties between the plantation master and his daughter was the talk and dismay of the family. The father frequently raised his hand in toasts to British soldiers, but the daughter could not forgive the Tories, and she championed the cause of Francis Marion and his men. It would be her fate to play an important part in a scenario involving Marion and his company of daredevil fighters.

Francis Marion, known as the Swamp Fox for his band of desperadoes who knew the geography of the inlets and marshes, was at his peak of performance during 1780 and 1781. He was receiving credit for holding the coastal area of South Carolina from the British, but, even with this success, he felt

Wedgefield Plantation Manor House   *Photo by Sid Rhyne*

some apprehension for the safety of his men. Finally, he convinced himself that the future was not as dismal as he had imagined, and his spirits lifted. As he perfected more and more theories of his particular style of warfare, his spirits soared. His tactics were working!

There was no more glorious moment in his military career, he felt, than the occasion when he discovered a camp of Tories relaxing, surely expecting nothing from the enemy. They laughed and joked, and some of them stretched out on the ground and fell asleep. The cagey Marion maneuvered his men into three groups, which he stationed around the camp. He told his men to get some rest, as they would make a surprise attack just as day was breaking.

At daybreak Marion held his pistol in the air and fired, giving the signal to strike. His men stormed the unsuspecting Tories from three sides. Within minutes the battle was over, and the loyalists that did not lie dead were moaning with wounds. From the stricken camp, Marion and his men took horses, saddles, bridles and muskets.

Marion knew about the little civil war in the mansions on the rivers. Fathers were divided against sons, brothers against brothers. It came as no surprise to the Swamp Fox when he received a message that the father of one of his men was being held prisoner at Wedgefield Plantation. It was the very thing the master of Wedgefield was likely to do, as he was a well-known supporter of the British. But his daughter? That was another matter.

As Marion sat under the low-hanging branches of an oak tree festooned in Spanish moss, he read a message from the daughter. She informed Marion that she was carrying out a plan to get the family away from the plantation and allow Marion and his men to come secretly in the night and free the prisoner. She advised Marion that she would place directions in the cemetery at Prince George Winyah Episcopal Church in Georgetown.

Naturally, such intrigue excited Marion. Especially did he desire to take advantage of the planter who was a Tory lover! And at the hand of the planter's own daughter. It was almost too good to be true.

The moonlit night was windy as Marion made his way along Highmarket Street, and turned left at the corner, at Broad. No one could see him, for he walked in the shadow of the brick wall enclosing the burial ground. Any cemetery is an eerie place at night, but as the wind howled on this night it carried with it its own leafy shrapnel that struck the shoulders of the man in a black suit and hat. Marion had chosen not to dress in full regalia in order to call no attention to himself.

He slipped through the gates into the cemetery and moved nimble-footedly among the white urns, carved stones and other symbols of death. Momentarily, his eyes fell on a child's grave, and he stooped down to examine the engraving on the marker. The wind in the trees threw moving shadows on the marble headstone that read:

LYDIA
Her youthful feet trod flowers that
bloom in beauty o'er her early tomb

On his knees now, Marion's hand went behind the small stone. Just as he had been secretly advised, a brick was propped against the grave marker. His fingers felt under the brick and found a note. Slipping it into a coat pocket, he quickly left the cemetery. When he reached camp, he lit a lamp and read the note.

Wedgefield Plantation

My dear Patriot,

I trust you received my last communication in
due time and that you desire to rescue the
prisoner held in our home. In good truth, I
perceive that no more appropriate time will
present itself for you to free the prisoner than
on Thursday next; we will attend a reception
at Mansfield Plantation, in the evening. I must
warn you that my father, whom I love
although his loyalties remain with England,
will leave a sentry on the veranda. From your
reputation as a leader of your company of men,
I rather expect the sentry will cause but little
opposition for you. It is not worth my while to
try to describe your means of retrieving this
man who is being held, for I have not the
language to do justice, and preparations occupy
me so entirely, and I am very much hurried
now as I expect to send my letter by Mr.
Delavillete, who is waiting for me to write.
Adieu.

> Your friend in the name of *succes
> d'estime* in the disputes between
> Great Britain and her colonies.

The following Thursday, Marion and his men galloped down
the avenue of oaks at Wedgefield Plantation. One of the horses
whinnied as it pranced to a stop. Under the portico lamp, the
sentry called, "Who's there?" Before he could draw his weapon,
one of Marion's men whacked off his head with a saber.

There was no immediate show of blood as the sword made a clean, instant severing of the head, which fell to the steps. Marion and his men rushed inside the mansion, freed the prisoner, and were gone.

Seven weeks later, in the moonlight, the ghost of the headless sentry was seen tottering in the garden. After that,especially on nights brightened by the moon, the apparition was noted as though searching for his head while he protected Wedgefield. Title to Wedgefield Plantation has changed over and over since Revolutionary times, but the watchman's ghost remained the same for many years, reeling and lurching in the garden on moonlit nights.

Note: Today Wedgefield Plantation is a residential community, but the manor house and abandoned rice fields can be seen. Wedgefield is located five miles north of Georgetown, just off U.S. 701. Look for the signs. The manor house dining room restaurant is open to the public.

The Man Who
Turned to Stone

"It just plain doesn't make any sense," a woman friend who was visiting the Blaskey family in Georgetown said.

"I'm with you," said another guest who was breaking bread with the family. "No mistake about it, to move the body of our dear friend from one location to another in the same cemetery, Elmwood, couldn't possibly matter." He blushed as he looked around and suddenly realized that none of the Blaskeys agreed with him. Their dear departed S. T. Blaskey had been a popular tailor in Georgetown before his death three years earlier. To soothe rivalries and to patch up differences in the family, all had finally agreed that the remains of S. T. Blaskey would be moved from the present burial plot in Elmwood Cemetery to one on the opposite side of the burial ground. Once they agreed on what they would do, each man at the table agreed to go to the cemetery two days later, on Wednesday, Feb. 23, 1910, and assist in digging up the casket and moving it to the desired location. There would be six men assisting in the operation, and by pulling together for the good of the whole, six men would provide ample strength.

The weather was mild for February on that Wednesday when family and friends set out for Elmwood Cemetery. This was a

Elmwood Cemetery in Georgetown *Photo by Sid Rhyne*

time when local banks were paying 5 percent interest on yearly deposits, and the Hunter's License Bill was being processed through the House of Representatives. Women used Royal Baking Powder when baking bread, and the Republicans were calling the cause of high prices a "bunco game." Senator Stone of Missouri spoke out plainly and warned the country of the whitewashing scheme proposed by the friends of a recently adopted tariff.

Arrangements for the transfer of the body had been made with the officials of the cemetery prior to the arrival of the six men, all of whom were carrying shovels.

As they dug away, removing the earth over the casket, one of the men suggested that they have a short service or at least a devotion, dedicated to the memory of S. T. But the others declined the suggestion and continued shoveling the Low Country sandy soil from the ground. The group's foresight had provided ropes with which to lift the casket from the ground.

Suddenly a shovel hit a hard object. They had reached the casket. After the soil had been removed from the top of the coffin, the men shoveled away the soil from the sides. Shot through with fresh vitality, the men went down on their knees and began to tunnel a passageway under the box for the ropes.

With the coffin securely tied with the ropes, the men straightened up. One, rubbing his kneecaps, mentioned that he trusted they could lift the object. A cemetery worker had already removed the earth from the new burial site, and a gaping hole was waiting on the opposite side of the burial ground.

At a count of three, the men — using all the strength they could muster — pulled on the ropes. The coffin wouldn't budge. "Challenging," one man noted with a sigh. The men pulled and pulled and finally concluded that more power was needed to lift the casket. A member of the party sent into town to summon help returned with three men. Surely nine strenuous men could lift S. T.'s remains.

Using all the energy and concentration they could command,
the men drew up the casket and pulled it to a clearing among
the graves and monuments. Panting heavily, they realized they
were barely a match for the heavy box. No way could they
transfer it to the other side of the cemetery without the use of a
horse-drawn wagon. They immediately sent for one. When it
arrived, the robust men gasped and hoisted the casket to the
wagon. The horse pulling the strange cargo was led slowly
through the small passages lined with marble monuments,
wreaths and other symbols of departed lives.

Just before S. T. Blaskey's casket was lowered into the new
grave, one of his friends said he would like to have a final look
at S. T. After all, they had been friends for a long time, and S. T.
had been dead only three years. The others mulled over the
suggestion, then agreed to lift the top of the coffin.

Three of the men lifted the top of the casket, and in brilliant
sunlight they all viewed S. T. He had turned to stone.

The men who had moved his body stood horror-stricken.
"He's petrified," one said, as he hesitantly reached out a hand,
then withdrew it as if unsure he should touch the petrified
corpse. Then he touched S. T., whose face was fully
recognizable. His clothing, although stone, had retained its
original color.

After each member of the party touched S. T. Blaskey, in
order to affirm with certainty what they were viewing, the
corpse was again laid to rest.

The following day newspapers across South Carolina carried
the story, with the following headlines:

Turned to Stone

*Body of Man Buried Three
Years Ago Petrified*

*Remains of S. T. Blaskey of Georgetown, When
Taken Up, Was Found to be a Solid Mass*

Note: Elmwood Cemetery in Georgetown is located at the corner of Highmarket and Hazard streets, one block from U.S. 17.

A Sinking Feeling

At the end of South Island Road in Georgetown, a road that leaves U.S. 17 south of the Sampit River Bridge, a ferry transports visitors from the mainland to the Yawkey Wildlife Center. It's not a haunted place, but it's worth a mention in a collection of stories dealing with bizarre activities and strange perceptions.

The Tom Yawkey Wildlife Center, willed to the South Carolina Wildlife and Marine Resources Department in 1976 by the late Tom Yawkey, is considered one of the most important gifts to wildlife conservation in North America. The center consists of three coastal islands — North, South and Cat — located in the mouth of Winyah Bay.

Tom Yawkey was a millionaire at the age of 16, becoming owner of family fortunes in mining, timber, tin and oil. When word of his inheritance came to him, he said, "I hope I'll be able to do some good with it. I hope I'll be as good a man as my dad."

Yawkey inherited the islands near Georgetown in 1919 from an uncle who owned the Detroit Tigers baseball club. The nephew took much the same path as the uncle, not only in revering the islands — he went on to buy the Boston Red Sox. With his millions, he could develop his islands as he chose, and he did just that. He believed that people and wildlife do not

The ferry crossing where the ferry carrying the power plant sank. *Photo by Sid Rhyne*

mix, and he elected to give wildlife the predominant use of the islands.

On these islands one can view flora and fauna much in the same state as it was a hundred and more years ago. Tom Yawkey made no secret of the fact that it was his wish that at least a part of the property would always be used as a wilderness area, which he defined as an area of undeveloped land retaining its primeval character and ecology.

Mr. and Mrs. Yawkey enjoyed visiting their wilderness islands where they could view many species of wild creatures. They took a special interest in the ospreys and eagles, wild turkeys and ducks, deer and alligators. Ruins of an old rice plantation, the Hume Plantation, brought nostalgic wonder to their imaginations.

During the mid years of this century, the Yawkeys frequently experienced worrisome periods when their source of electricity was knocked out by electrical storms. Their islands were especially susceptible to the hurricanes that swept in on ocean tides. Finally, Yawkey decided to have a private power plant built for his islands. He contacted Westinghouse and asked for a top-flight engineer who would be willing to come to Georgetown, look over the situation, and counsel him on such an undertaking. The engineer who was given the assignment was a knowledgeable man, a graduate of MIT.

Yawkey discussed the construction of his power plant with the young engineer and warned him that when it was completed, it would be necessary that it come to the island by barge, traveling by way of the Intracoastal Waterway.

"When the power plant comes," Yawkey cautioned, "it cannot be transported over the water by the ferry. That ferry just won't support such equipment."

But the engineer insisted that the ferry *would* support the power plant. "I'm the engineer," he boasted, "and *I* should be the one to say how the equipment will be moved over water. The ferry will absolutely support the unit that I will design."

The engineer returned home to work on Yawkey's project. Yawkey was worried, knowing that if the engineer demanded that the power plant be sent over on the ferry, the vessel would surely sink to the bottom of the Waterway. Yawkey got in touch with the engineer and further asserted that he should give some thought to a barge rather than the ferry. "I just have a sinking feeling that the ferry won't hold up," Yawkey said. But the engineer could not be swayed.

Finally, Yawkey was informed of the day of the arrival of his power plant. He felt in his heart of hearts that there would be a disaster on that day. Again he contacted the engineer and demanded that the generator be transported by barge, but to no avail. "The ferry will be quite sufficient, I'm sure," the engineer said.

Yawkey contacted newspaper reporters from Georgetown, Myrtle Beach and Charleston, notifying them of the arrival of his power plant. Reporters and photographers who swarmed to the scene were surprised to see that Yawkey had provided a sumptuous buffet for them to enjoy while they awaited the arrival of the generator. Champagne flowed freely, and it was accompanied by the finest of caviar. While they feasted, Yawkey warned them that they were in for a surprise. His power plant, he said, would sink into the waterway. Cameras were set to record the unlikely event.

After a while, a rumbling sound was heard. "There it comes," yelled Yawkey, pointing to a flatbed truck. The power plant was on the truck.

The engineer, traveling with the generator, shouted greetings to Yawkey.

"I'm giving you one last chance," Yawkey said, a glass of champagne in his hand. "You don't have to go through with this. We can still get a barge."

The engineer brushed him aside. "I know what I'm doing. I'm the man who designed this equipment, and I'll be the man who transports it to the island and secures it in place."

Yawkey settled down with the reporters and photographers while the power plant was being loaded onto the ferry. The vessel left land and drifted onto the wide, boisterous Intracoastal Waterway. Just as it reached the midway point, the ferry began to ride lower and lower in the water. Soon, water washed over the deck and the new power plant was sinking out of sight. The cameras were clicking.

Yawkey held his glass of champagne high in the air and called to the engineer, "You must go down with the equipment! Every good captain goes down with his ship!" But the engineer jumped overboard and swam to shore.

Note: According to Robert L. Joyner, Superintendent of the Tom Yawkey Wildlife Center, Tom Yawkey refused to accept delivery of the power plant after it had been saturated with salt water, and a new generator was built. It is used today as an auxiliary generator when the power from the local electric company is knocked out by a storm.

To inquire about a visit to the Tom Yawkey Wildlife Center, write to Robert L. Joyner, Tom Yawkey Wildlife Center, Route 2, Georgetown, South Carolina 29440.

Hampton Plantation

Hampton Plantation, located 17 miles south of Georgetown on Rutledge Road, two miles west of U.S. 17 (look for the sign on the right of the highway after crossing the South Santee River), is one of the most magnificent of Low Country plantations. None in *Gone With The Wind* is a match for this place, in beauty or historical connections.

Hampton House was built in the 1730s by Huguenots who had settled on the South Santee River. Daniel Horry (Oh-ree) owned other plantations but chose Hampton as his country seat. His second wife was Harriott Pinckney, the only daughter of Eliza and Charles Pinckney. Harriott and Daniel had two children. Their daughter Harriott married Frederick Rutledge and began the line that would own the property until 1970, when Archibald Rutledge chose to sell the plantation to the state of South Carolina for $150,000. Rutledge wrote many books about Hampton and his life on the plantation. Probably his most famous book is *Home By The River* (Sandlapper Publishing Co., 1983).

Visitors are welcomed here. You can stand on the porch where Harriott Horry adjusted her sash and skirts as she awaited Gen. George Washington, or go into the ballroom where Washington ate breakfast, or stand by the fireplace in the drawing room where Francis Marion rested until the sound of hooves believed to be bringing enemy soldiers urged him to make a fast getaway, or stand on the veranda where a funeral was held on Sept. 15, 1973, for Archibald Rutledge. He was buried in the family cemetery in the garden. Will Alston, a man who is a descendant of people born in slavery and who still works at Hampton, summed up the feelings of all who knew Dr. Rutledge when he said of Sept. 15, 1973, "That was a broken-hearted day."

The Hampton Ghost

A motorcoach, carrying a bevy of travelers from a northern state, turned into the Hampton Plantation gate and made its way under low-hanging limbs to a parking lot/rest area. When the group had made their way up the grassy incline to the mansion looming in the sun, they were met by Robert Mitchell, Superintendent of Hampton Plantation State Park. Mitchell is a no-nonsense young man who takes seriously the history and folklore of this renowned plantation under his supervision. After standing on the veranda and recalling the funeral of the late Dr. Archibald Rutledge, held on this very porch, he led the group into the ballroom.

The Hampton ballroom is one of the most impressive ballrooms in the Western Hemisphere, and it owes much of its prominence and prestige to Harriott Pinckney Horry who was mistress of Hampton after her marriage to Daniel Horry on Feb. 15, 1768. Harriott played the part of a glamorous First Lady, as she entertained the most noble in the land, including George Washington.

From the ballroom, Mitchell, as he lectured, walked ahead of the visitors, and they ascended the stairs and approached a room on the right of the stairway. Just as Mitchell started to give some information on that room, a woman in the group slapped her hand over her mouth and mumbled something. She was obviously all but overtaken with fear.

She told Mitchell that she had an extraordinary measure of extrasensory perception and that there was a "presence" in that room. It frightened her, she said, and she refused to enter the room and demanded that she be escorted back downstairs. Mitchell did not hesitate to hold her arm as she made her way to the first floor, for he well knew that John Henry Rutledge had committed suicide in that room and his presence was believed to be as much a part of the room as the windows and door.

When the woman was safely on the veranda, heaving a deep sigh of relief, Mitchell went upstairs and continued his lecture and tour of the mansion. But his thoughts were on the woman downstairs, and how she had been perceptive enough to notice the presence that he and Will Alston had so often discussed as they worked on the plantation said to be the "granddaddy" of other coastal South Carolina plantations.

In the golden age of Old South plantations, none was more golden than Hampton. The mansion, believed to have been

Hampton Plantation   *Photo by Sid Rhyne*

built by a French immigrant about the middle of the eighteenth century, has for more than two hundred years been a museum of plantation life that no Hollywood studio could duplicate. The white mansion rises above the South Santee River, above the deer herds that come to the meadows to feast, above moss-draped live oak trees that are hundreds of years old, and seemingly soars for the sky. But one of the most outstanding features was the Rutledge family, granted immortality by their social, political and literary pursuits. Not to mention that they were fabulously wealthy. Hampton Plantation was a pleasure and treasure place, and today it's a kind of shrine to the Rutledges and Horrys.

Daniel Horry was a widower, having outlived his wife and children, when he married the lovely Harriott Pinckney. Harriott's parents had already become the trendsetters of that day, and they were pleased with the union of their daughter and the owner of Hampton. Harriott's mother, Eliza Pinckney, was a beautiful redhead, and when she expressed delight when Harriott said she might visit for some length of time, Harriott answered in fluent French, "Il n'y a pas de quoi." Harriott and Eliza knew and practiced the social graces of entertaining and were considered the leading hostesses of the South. However, they saw to it that Harriott's children, Daniel and Harriott, received stringent instruction in certain skills, habits, values and attitudes.

Daniel, endowed with the relentless coaching of his mother and grandmother, pleased them in most that he did, but never more than when he "married well," taking for his wife Elenore Marie Florimonde de Fay La Tour Marbourg, a niece of the celebrated Marquis de Lafayette. But daughter Harriott, who was not the beauty that her mother and grandmother were, seemed destined not to marry. It was the custom for women of that day to marry young, and Harriott was well into her twenties and still a spinster. It came as quite a surprise to the elder

Harriott when she received word that her daughter had eloped with Frederick Rutledge. As Rutledge was a "good name," a symbol of "the quality," the family was quite pleased to have the Rutledge name linked with the Hampton tradition.

Harriott and Frederick Rutledge had eight children, four girls and four boys, including John Henry. When John Henry Rutledge became a man, he fell in love with the daughter of a pharmacist. He told his mother about his love for the young girl, and she was outraged. He must, she said, find a girl equal more to the station of the Rutledges of Hampton.

At first John Henry fumed, then he became angry, but finally his anger filtered into a state of depression. He spent most of his time in a room on the second floor at the top of the stairs. It was in this room that the exquisite leather-bound books of Hampton were kept. But John Henry did not glance at the books. He sat in a rocking chair and cried and moaned and wailed. He couldn't accept his mother's criteria for a wife for him, as it was his conviction that any man should be allowed to marry the woman of his choice, whether or not she was considered to be of the quality.

The rest of the family ignored John Henry, believing that he would come out of his depression and find a girl more suitable to his lifestyle. But that was not to be. John Henry did leave Hampton for a short while, in order to pay a call on the father of the girl he wished to marry. The girl's father told him that although he, John Henry, was ill, he, as a pharmacist, could not treat a broken heart. He suggested that John Henry forget about his daughter, because he had no intention of allowing her to marry a Rutledge. His daughter would never, absolutely never, be allowed to move to Hampton and be regarded as inferior to the other members of the family.

In March of 1830, as he sat in the rocking chair in the upstairs library, John Henry shot himself with a sawed-off shotgun. His body slumped, then fell to the floor near the doorway. (This was the very room the woman on the tour refused to enter because of a presence.)

John Henry Rutledge was buried in the garden on the river side of the house, and a plain white marble slab was placed over his final resting place. It reads:

In Memory
of
John Henry Rutledge
Son of
Frederick and Harriott (Horry) Rutledge
who departed this life
on the 5th of March 1830
aged 21 years
He was distinguished for
Fortitude & firmness
The Goodness & the magnanimity that he
showed even in the agonies of a painful
Death made indelible impressions upon
all who witnessed it
He died in Peace with all men & in the full
Confidence that his Maker would receive
his Soul with that Mercy & forgiveness
which is the hope & solace of the Penitent
in his approach to the throne of the Eternal

Several years after the death of John Henry Rutledge, a servant at Hampton heard a chair rocking in the upstairs library. She flew up the stairs to investigate, and although the chair was steadily rocking, no one could be seen in it. She called a member of the Rutledge family to come and look, who saw that though there was no apparent propulsion by any person or thing, the chair rocked as though someone were sitting in the chair, propelling it to rock. As they left the room — with the chair still rocking — they could hear muffled sounds almost like a man crying and bemoaning the fact that he was unable to marry his true love. For years, members of the Rutledge family and their servants heard the sad sounds coming from the upstairs library, and the chair continued to rock, although it was always empty.

In later years, after Sue Alston began working at Hampton (Archibald Rutledge was to refer to her as "the guardian angel of Hampton"), she noticed a bloodlike stain on the floor by the rocking chair. She scrubbed the floor and cleaned it of the stain and went back downstairs. But a few hours later, the bloodstain was back. She again cleaned the floor, and again the bloodstain came back. As Sue's children grew, they were given certain tasks at Hampton, and Sue's son, Will, helped her in the mansion. Will Alston works at Hampton today, and he will tell anyone who talks with him about his mother and himself scrubbing the floor in the room where John Henry Rutledge killed himself, but the bloodstains returned, time after time. "After we cleaned that floor, the blood just pumped back up," Will says. Finally, after years and years of scrubbing, the bloodstain did not return. (Sue Alston died in December, 1983 at the age of 110.)

Through the years, there have been other strange goings-on in the Hampton library, as well as the empty chair that rocked. There are unidentifiable noises, especially when the mist comes in from the sea and saturates the moss that hangs from the oak trees, and when a big storm blows in, the ghost closes the windows! You can go and see for yourself. Hampton Plantation State Park is open from daylight to dark, seven days a week, and the mansion is open to the public for a nominal fee from 10 AM to 3 PM on Saturdays, and from 12 Noon to 3 PM on Sundays.

The Sweetest Legend
of Hampton

Few people experience a love for their home that the late Dr. Archibald Rutledge felt for Hampton Plantation, which he referred to as his home by the river, the home of his ancestors. Rutledge was poet laureate of South Carolina, and he wrote many books. In one of them he said he believed it was worthwhile to record the many adventures that had befallen him at Hampton, and I believe that this adventure is the sweetest of all the Hampton legends. It concerns Christmas at Hampton Plantation.

Elaborate preparations were made to decorate the mansion with native greens, and a few days before Christmas Day, the men in the family were sent into the forest to fetch armfuls of mistletoe, hollies, pine, cedar and wild smilax. After their return, women servants sat on the floor of the pillared verandah and made garlands of greenery, using an old-time method of making green ropes from the strongly scented cedar, pine and other growth. The garlands were draped from the corners of the ballroom ceiling and on the stair railing in the hallway. Mistletoe was everywhere.

A cedar tree about two stories high was stationed before the fireplace in the ballroom, and decorations consisted of rope

made from beads, colored paper, popped corn. Other or-
naments consisted of decorations made of wood.

Christmas Eve came, and Sue Alston, Rutledge's "guardian
angel of Hampton," was cooking a ham in the outdoor kitchen.
It took nearly an entire day to prepare the ham. First she boiled
it in a huge black pot of water. Then she baked it in the oven.
Finally, she took it to the pantry in the big house and sliced it,
carefully layering the slices on a silver tray. Sue also cooked
duck and wild turkeys, which had been taken by the men who
hunted in the woods. Sue was later to speak of the cake that
she made for Christmas. It was covered with white icing and
garnished with red berries. Guests were always present at
Christmastime, and it was her duty to see that food awaited
them on the groaning board. More than enough.

During the afternoon of this day, Christmas Eve, Rutledge sat
on the steps and talked with his friend, Prince Alston. Prince
was Sue's husband. Rutledge had a special fondness for Prince,
for they were the same age and had been comrades for as long
as Rutledge could remember.

That day they talked about Christmas legends. "Have you
heard the one about the animals on Christmas, at the time of
Jesus' birth?" Rutledge asked. Prince said that he had, and he
believed it perfectly. He never doubted that on Christmas Eve,
every living bird and animal goes down on its knees in adora-
tion of the newborn master at the stroke of midnight.

When the conversation ended, Prince walked through the
grove of oaks called the Pretty Woods to his home, and
Rutledge went inside the mansion. It was magnificent in fresh
greenery. There was a strong fragrance of pine and cedar, and a
fire roared on the hearth.

Finally, everyone was called to dinner, and the groaning board
was laden with every conceivable food that could be prepared
at Hampton. The table gleamed with English china, and silver

and crystal. Archibald Rutledge gave thanks to the Lord for his
blessings and mercies, and then the family ate until they were
fairly stuffed.

After dinner, and as the evening waned, Rutledge went to the
verandah to enjoy the velvet sky and blazing stars. He'd never
seen the sky more magnificent. It must have been such a night
as this when Jesus was born. He thought about the legend of
the animals and wondered if it could possibly be true that they
paid homage to the Christ child at midnight. Prince Alston
believed it, but he was snugly home in his cabin with Sue and
their children. As he thought more about it, Rutledge decided
to test the story. How could any animal be aware of the birth of
the baby Jesus, much less be inspired to go down on its knees at
midnight?

Rutledge made his way down the steps. As he walked toward
the stableyard he was almost unable to take his eyes off the
sky. Never had he seen it so brilliant. The stars seemed larger
than he'd ever seen them, and they looked to be almost
suspended, not so far away. Then a movement caught his eye,
and he noticed his friend Prince Alston sitting there in the
stableyard, under a pine tree.

"Why, Prince, I didn't expect to see you here."

"Boss, I not spec to see you here."

"What are you looking for, Prince?"

"Well, it soon be midnight, the time when little baby Jedus
be borned. I be here to see the old ox, and the hogs and the
sheeps."

"We have about five minutes to wait," Rutledge answered.
"Then we'll see what happens." He sat down beside his friend,
and for a few minutes they discussed their deep religious feelings and their reverence for Christmastime.

Just then a rooster crowed with uncommon vigor, and all the
other roosters in the vicinity joined him. "Lissen," Prince said.

"The animals are getting ready to honor the birth of Jedus."

"You could be right," Rutledge answered. "I've always believed that was only a legend, but it could be true after all."

And just then the sheep in a pen beyond the stable began to bleat in a strange form, as though they were expressing compassion.

"I've never heard the like of this," Rutledge said, as a pig squealed, and then another.

And as Rutledge and Prince listened, the huge old ox began to stir.

"Look!" Prince exclaimed.

"I'm looking, Prince."

In a moment the hind quarters of the ox were up, but his head was so low it was almost on the ground.

"Prince, do you know what the ox is doing?" Rutledge asked.

"I know. He be kneeling."

"Precisely. He is kneeling in sacredness at the very moment of the birth of our Savior."

"All the animals on this plantation be honoring their Maker," Prince answered.

And it was true.

Charleston

Roots go deep here, in spirit, in culture, in family heritage. Charles Town and the surrounding coastal Low Country first were settled by the English in 1670. Dependent from the start on slave labor, great plantations producing indigo, rice and cotton thrived in the early eighteenth century. Some of the great plantations are in existence today. Many of the townhouses and churches of the planters stand in Charleston.

Charleston today is perhaps the most proud and self-possessed city in the United States. This town has been called the historical center of the nation, and houses facing the famous Battery, a sturdy seawall, have been referred to as having "America's Most Prestigious Address." Right or wrong, Charlestonians revere the city as a kind of holy place.

Charleston is waterbound by two rivers, the Cooper and the Ashley, and the harbor is noted even in England for its beauty. Charleston children are taught that "this is the city where the Cooper and Ashley rivers meet to form the Atlantic Ocean."

On the streets of the historic section, near the Battery, you will discover one architectural treasure after another. The city has more than 70 buildings that predate the Revolution, more than 200 built before the war of 1812, and more than 850 constructed before the Civil War. An eighteenth-century flavor pervades all of it.

Extraordinary restaurants, featuring local specialties, and gift shops are in the area of The Old Market that extends from Meeting Street nearly to the Cooper River. By continuing on Meeting Street to the bay, you will see the famous Battery and the stately old mansions facing the bay. Fort Sumter is located in the bay, and sightseeing boats transport visitors there.

Charleston is reached from the Grand Strand by traveling U.S. 17 South.

The Ghost in
St. Philips Graveyard

The first Anglican Church organized south of Virginia was St. Philips, and it is the oldest church organization in Charleston today.

In 1670 the colonists settled at a point west of the Ashley River, which they called "Old Town," and although they worshipped in that section of Charles Town — named for King Charles II of England — no church sanctuary was constructed there. Later on, they moved to a place called Oyster Point, in the area known today as the Historic Section, and constructed a church on the site of St. Michael's Episcopal Church, on Meeting Street. Vestrymen were kept busy recording the names of new members; by 1710 the membership had fairly exploded, and the vestrymen decided the construction of a new church was in order. The new church was built of brick on the present-day site of St. Philips, on Church Street.

The colonists were a careful people, rather afraid of originality. They patterned their new church after the Jesuit Church in Antwerp, said to be a building of ideal proportion and mystifying beauty. On completion, St. Philips was called "the most elegant religious edifice in America." Boatmen on the nearby docks came to use the beautiful church as a landmark and said

St. Philips Church and graveyard.

Photo: Charleston Chamber of Commerce

it bore a certain resemblance to the medieval idea of heaven. It was 100 feet long, 60 feet wide and 40 feet high, with a cupola of 50 feet, which housed two bells and a clock. Although the boatmen and dockworkers revered St. Philips, they did not attend services there. Most of them were slaves, and some of them were owned by the wealthy planters whose names were on St. Philips's membership roll. The rich planters were primarily Episcopalian, as Episcopal rectors did not frown on slavery.

Charles Town was a port of entry, and schooners from the river plantations came into the port where their products, usually indigo and rice, were unloaded and sold. The products were then shipped to England or other points around the world. Shipping in Charles Town also consisted of steamers traveling from New York to the West Indies, by way of this port city. There were also vessels on a New York to Charles Town run.

A slave named Boney worked at the docks, unloading the rice that was sent down to Charles Town by his master, the owner of a Waccamaw River plantation. Boney lived in a small house at the back of his master's Charles Town mansion on King Street. Most of Boney's work was done during the daylight hours, when his master's schooners arrived in Charles Town to be unloaded. But often, Boney hung around the docks at night.

Boney's master brought his vessels down to Charles Town by "the ocean route," and Boney could recognize the schooners as they entered the bay, coming in from the ocean. The people on the docks said Boney had the clearest vision of any other person in the town, and Boney believed it too. Not only could he detect details from a long distance, but he could make out specific people on board the schooners, even when the days were overcast and light was poor. As time went on, Boney became known for his keen eyesight, and he believed his vision was amplified.

One night in 1796, Boney was on the dock checking out the

facilities, as he knew that his master was sending down two schooners of rice the following morning. He had alerted the factor, who served as a banker and stockbroker for the planter. The factor also worked for other planters, some of whom sent rice in rough form to Charles Town. The factor would direct the vessels carrying rough rice to the wharves of the McLaren mill where the rice would be cleaned of husks and therefore bring a higher price. Boney's master had his own rice mill on the Waccamaw River, and the rice was clean when it arrived in Charles Town. Because it was ready for market, the rice brought a high price. After the factor sold the rice that belonged to Boney's master, he invested the money in stocks of the United States Bank or the Bank of Charles Town. Boney's master was a millionaire.

Boney was talking with the factor that night, chatting about the schooners of clean rice that would arrive the next morning. The factor was friendly to Boney because the factor had become a wealthy man from the rice he sold for Boney's master. That night the talk got around to Boney's freedom.

Boney said he desired his freedom more than any other slave he knew, but that it was unlikely he would receive it. He was aware of his value to his master, and although "Marse Robert" was a man of integrity, he would never consider letting Boney go free. Then he spoke of a slave named Caesar who had obtained his freedom after he had perfected an antidote for rattlesnake bite. Caesar had worked out a concoction of plantain, hoarhound and golden rod roots, compounded with rum and lye, and then wrapped in tobacco leaves that had been soaked in rum. In 1750 the legislature had ordered his prescription published for the benefit of the public. The Charles Town journal printed it and found its copies exhausted by the demand.

"Boney, do you think you can do something that will bring you fame and freedom?" the factor asked.

"No," Boney answered, solemnly. But he didn't know that through his sharp and unusual vision, he would do something that very night that would bring him his freedom.

As Boney talked to the factor, he faced St. Philips Church steeple. He stopped listening to what the factor was saying and squinted his eyes in the direction of the church.

"What is it, Boney?" the factor asked.

"Don't rightly know, but it seem to me there be a fire in the steeple."

The factor looked in the direction of the church steeple. "There's no fire there, Boney. All is dark up there."

"No. Fire be there sho nuf," Boney said as he broke into a run in the direction of the church.

Boney ran as fast as he could, his heart pumping hard against his chest. When he reached the brick church on Church Street, he started climbing up the side of the building. His nimble fingers felt for any outcropping of brick that he could clasp. Slipping back a little, now and then, he held fast and did not fall to the ground. Finally, he reached the wood steeple, but it was necessary for him to climb still further to the roof of this spire. Boney kept the cross on the very tip of the ornamental structure in his vision as he climbed past the bells, then past the clock. He could see a cedar shingle burning. But for the life of him, he couldn't figure out how a fire had started there. If he didn't reach it soon, the blaze would spread to other shingles, and the historic church would be engulfed in flames.

Boney reached the top, and he pulled with all his strength to dislodge the burning shingle. His hands were burned as he at last pulled the slab from the pegs holding it in place. He threw the burning shingle into the air, in the direction of the Cooper River. Then, with one hand, he tore the shirt from his body and smothered the tongue of fire that was licking other shingles. When the fire was out and all was dark, Boney made his way down the building. At the bottom, the factor and a group of dockworkers stood, watching. They told Boney that he had saved the building from destruction.

When Boney's master arrived in Charleston the next morning, the factor told him what had happened. The master thought about it for a while, and then he summoned Boney to stop working and come to him. Boney couldn't believe he was hearing the words correctly when the master gave him his freedom. "If ever any deed deserved to bring the gift of freedom," the master said, "this one does. For I was married in that church."

Boney left the dock and went home and told his wife and children the good news. He never worked again, but he spent the rest of his days hanging around St. Philips Church, especially in the adjacent burial ground. Boney sat, hours on end, his back resting on a grave marker, his gaze fixed on the steeple.

Although Boney had desired emancipation, he was unable to adjust to his freedom. He wanted to be on the docks, working with the people whom he knew. This thing called *freedom* wasn't the best thing in the world as he had once believed. Boney lost weight until he had almost withered away, and when death came, he was laid to rest in the slave cemetery on his master's Waccamaw River plantation.

The cornerstone of the present St. Philips Church building was laid on Nov. 12, 1835. The steeple, designed by Edward B. White, was added about 1848-50. The bells were removed from the steeple in 1862 and given to the Confederacy to be used in making cannon. The church was damaged in that war.

One evening as a Charleston woman who held exceptional hereditary rank and privilege in Charleston rode on Church Street in her carriage, she noted something in the cemetery at St. Philips, something most unusual. She had her driver stop the carriage, and she got out and walked into the burial ground where so many famous people had been given their final resting place. As she meandered among the monuments and markers, she didn't notice anything amiss, and she began to think of the distinguished and prominent leaders buried there. They included some of the early provincial governors of the Province of South Carolina; Edward Rutledge, a signer of the Declaration of Independence; John C. Calhoun; and some Episcopal bishops. Just as she was about to leave, from a corner of her eye she noticed a movement among the markers. Walking a little hesitantly in that direction, she made out the form of a man who appeared to be a slave. He sat with his back resting against a marker. And with the most intense stare, he gazed at the steeple. His skin and hair were dark, but his eyes were the most remarkable color, or noncolor. They seemed almost white in their unwavering gaze. The matron returned to her home and told the details of the experience to her children.

There have been sightings of "a gray man" in the cemetery at St. Philips on several occasions. Does Boney hang out there, gazing at the steeple?

Note: DuBose Heyward, author of *Porgy*, is among the celebrated people who were buried in St. Philips cemetery.

The Ghost
at Charleston's City Hall

In thoroughbred Charleston, where the people of the city put a lot of backing into heritage and tradition, a thoroughbred ghost walks the halls of a government-owned and operated building — city hall.

The city hall is strategically situated on the northeast corner of Meeting and Broad streets, at what is known as the "Four Corners of Law." Other buildings at this intersection are the courthouse, post office, and St. Michaels Church. This corner, they say, is regulated by the laws of three governments — federal, county, municipal — and God. Of these commanding edifices, St. Michaels Church is the most noted and revered. It was designed by Sir Christopher Wren and built sometime between 1759 and 1781. The spire is 180 feet high, and it is considered to be the principal point in Charleston.

Within the walls of the city hall walks the resident ghost, who, even by Charleston standards, is a star in the heritage of the quality. Although the ghost is the spirit of one who was not of the South Carolina Low Country bloodlines, he came, he saw, and he remained — at least in spirit. Charleston has great affection for the spirit of General Pierre Gustave Toutant de Beauregard, Confederate general in the U.S. Civil War, who lurks in the shadows of city hall corridors.

Charleston's City Hall — a ghost roams the halls.

Photo: Charleston Chamber of Commerce

The proud, New Orleans-born Beauregard had all of Charleston at his feet during the time of the Civil War. Whisperings in the damasked drawing rooms and candlelighted fashionable taverns, frequented by the aristocratic Low Country society, were of the dapper gentleman.

"Beauregard's true name is Toutant," one said, the second week of April, 1861. "He took this other fine one from a plantation that was once among his holdings."

"Just now they say he is horribly depressed," another murmured. "In addition to all this talk of war, his wife, Caroline Deslonde, is ill in New Orleans."

Above the breathy talk, a strident voice announced, "He is sickened over Governor Pickens's wife's extravagances. Oh, he bows to the flush of youth of Lucy Holcombe, now Mrs. Governor Pickens. But we all know that she is a consummate actress. Why, she even offered Beauregard a violet from her breastpin."

"Did he accept it?"

"Well, don't laugh up your sleeve at it, but he did accept the violet, much in the part of a male flirt, I might add. But it's truly believed that like the rest of us, Beauregard detests her unrestrained waste."

"Waste?"

"Her excessiveness, my dear. In dresses that twirl as she dances in the arms of men," came the hushed reply.

"And her *three* servants, always hovering around her in public, and her violets. She's the governor's third wife. From Texas. They were married in 1858. But happiness is eluding him as she drives him further into debt."

Other bits of secret information passed from one to another as the women dined on pate de foie gras, salad, biscuit glace and champagne frappe.

The Charleston matrons lifted their skirts, and they swished and rustled out of the cafe and back to the iron gates of their mansions on the Battery. But they got no sleep that night. The streets became alive with soldiers shouting and ammunition wagons rumbling on the cobblestones. Governor Pickens and General Beauregard held a council of war.

The next day, word came that Fort Sumter would be fired upon at four o'clock if terms were not accepted. The chimes at St. Michaels Church pealed over the city, forewarning of imminent danger.

Four o'clock came. There was a volley of cannon fire. The women in the Battery-front palaces ran to the rooftops to view the beginning of the Civil War from their widows' walks atop the structures. They could not tell what destruction each volley accomplished.

"God is on our side," Adele Whaley cried, as the streets filled with aides in swords and red sashes, running to and fro. "He hates the Yankees!"

The Charleston women were forced to settle down and spend their time sitting idly, looking out over the harbor and wondering if anything would ever be the same again.

Fort Sumter surrendered, and the misfortune made Beauregard sacred to Charlestonians. It was the second calamity that would bring him laudatory notice.

It was just before the pomp and circumstance of the war that a man who was a member of the bluest of the Charleston bluebloods was given a large amount of money in bank notes. The money belonged to the state, and the man had been asked to deposit it in a bank on Broad Street. But he didn't go straight to the bank. That night he put the roll on a walnut bedside table, locked himself in his room, and slept the sleep of the moral, upright Charlestonians. The next morning, he discovered that the money was gone!

All the people of Charleston believed him, of course, because he was a Presbyterian. In spite of his character, Beauregard sped to the mansion and began a search. All the while, the upright citizen was bawling and squalling, proclaiming his innocence in a most un-Presbyterian way.

Beauregard searched nearly all day but could not find the money. Finally, he decided to remove the wainscot from the wall, and there, behind the cypress paneling, was the money. Beauregard raced to city hall, all the while murmuring what if the rats had gotten to the bank notes.

It is remembered that the bluebloods of Charleston elevated General Beauregard to the pedestal of the righteous, for he never once damaged the character of the man who hid the money by exposing him to ridicule. No cloud rested on Beauregard for the rest of his years. But the ghost of General Beauregard still roams the corridors of city hall, watching, they say, lest another member of the quality should hide a pile of money behind the wainscot.

Note: The entrance stairs at the Broad Street entry to city hall are referred to as the open arms stairway, because one set of steps circles to the left and the other set circles to the right from the street to the entrance.

The Haunted
Avenue of Oaks

Three miles from Charleston, on the properties of the Charleston Naval Base by the Cooper River, stands an avenue of ancient live oaks. The ghost of a slave girl haunts the passageway between the huge trees. She awaits a slave boy whom she believed would free her by sailing away from the plantation's Cooper River landing. So overtaken with grief was she at the rejection of her friend, that she burned the mansion, Belvidere, on the hill that overlooked the Cooper River.

It was here that the slave boy pushed his boat from the shore and fled on the Cooper River.

Photo Credit: PHAN Mike Mummert

The *South Carolina Historical and Genealogical Magazine* (6:98) contains this passage:

> BELVIDERE. — The handsome estate . . . was formerly the home of Thomas Shubrick. The present house was built about the end of the 18th., or beginning of the 19th., century, as the following extract from *The City Gazette & Daily Advertiser* for Tuesday, March 22, 1796, shows that a former dwelling on the same estate was burned in 1796: "Belvidere, the elegent seat of Thomas Shubrick, esq. three miles from this city, was yesterday morning destroyed by fire. We are informed that all the furniture, except what was in the lower story, was consumed."

How the plantation got its name is found in the *South Carolina Historical and Genealogical Magazine* (12:46).

> In 1712 the General Assembly of the Province authorized the sale to Governor Robert Johnson of a tract of land and a house on it, commonly called "the Governor's House." The tract of land was purchased by Governor Robert Johnson, from the General Assembly, and the tract and house later was known as Belvidere. After Johnson's death it became the seat of Governor Glen (probably by purchase from Gabriel Manigualt, who acquired himself by purchase most of Johnson's landed property) and after Glen's departure from the Province it passed to Thomas Shubrick, whom we find in possession. In Shubrick's hands it was known as Belvidere.

The same record verifies that toward the end of the Proprietorial Era this property became the site of the Governor's House, an official residence of English governors of the Province. At the end of the eighteenth century, while it belonged to Colonel Thomas Shubrick, the old residence was burned. The Shubricks replaced it with a very fine example of the Low Country's Adam-style architecture.

For many years, Belvidere handsomely housed the Charleston Country Club, and its fields sloping down to the Cooper River were the site of a golf course. The house has been destroyed, but the haunted avenue of oaks remain, as a part of the Charleston Naval Base.

In those days, the lesser folk enjoyed their fairs and cockfighting and the baiting of bears, while the planter families frequented horse races in Charleston and the wonderful balls that followed them. The owner of the winner of the race took home "a very fashionable piece of silver," and in order to race the finest horses that could be obtained, the planters searched everywhere. Many yearlings were bought in Virginia, some costing in the thousands of dollars.

On the day of the race, the owner and his horses went to the track quite early in the day, and the wives and daughters arrived later, amid much pomp and circumstance. They rode in fine carriages, some bearing the coat of arms of the family, and pulled by four matching bay horses. The ladies were dressed in the most exquisite jewels that Paris had to offer. Horse racing was one of the ingredients that kept the planter society so closely knit. Many horses belonging to the planters of Georgetown County, all of whom owned elaborate townhouses in Charleston, won races. Dr. John Murray's horse Skim won a race, as did William Alston's horse, Tryal.

One day as the Shubricks were preparing for a race at the Jockey Club in Charleston, a young slave girl approached a dark man who was placing oyster shells in the garden to form walkways.

"I be just the one to get you all the Missus' jewels if you take me away from Belvidere in that boat down at the landing."

"What you say, gal?" He stopped working in the shells.

"Fore sunrise, tomorrow. Right down there at the landing. You have boat ready. I run till I fall, but I'll have the Missus' jewels. You be a rich man from that day on."

"You mean you get the Missus' jewels and give to me and we leave Belvidere?"

"Just you think how good it gonna feel to be free. And to have them jewels. And be rich like Marse and Missus."

"It make my skin be prickly and the flesh crawl on the back of my neck to think about it," he answered, skeptically.

"You be there fore first light. I'll have the jewels."

The slave girl was Mrs. Shubrick's body servant, and when Mrs. Shubrick returned from a ball she was always there to help her Missus with her jewelry and clothes. After Mr. Shubrick had returned from the ball that followed the race at the Jockey Course, Mrs. Shubrick laid her jewelry on her bed. There was a bracelet made of links of gold, and within each link was an emerald. Her necklace held a huge ruby, encircled with diamonds, and there was a tiara of the most brilliant diamonds. As Mrs. Shubrick removed a black pearl ring set in platinum, she asked the slave girl to put the jewelry in the velvet box. She said she would later place it in the family vault, which she kept in an armoire on the second floor. The girl quickly dropped the jewelry in her apron pockets and filled the velvet box with rocks, which she had put in her pockets for that very purpose. After that, she walked downstairs, out of the house and into the avenue of oaks, and went to her cabin in the servants' quarters.

The following morning, before first light, she flew to the

Cooper River landing, the jewels still in the pockets of her apron. The Missus had not discovered the theft, she thought.

The young boy was in the small boat. "You got the jewels?"

"I got em. And they'd have a time catching me. I covered that ground fast." She held the apron in such a way that the jewels could not fall out of the pockets.

The boy climbed up on the dock. He spread a piece of cloth on the floor. "Put them there. Let me see. You could be fooling me."

The girl dumped the jewels on the cloth, and the boy scooped up the cloth quickly, jumped into the boat and was out of sight before the girl knew what was happening. She didn't even have time to say anything.

The slave girl was desperate. She knew that the theft would be discovered soon — there was another horse race that day. For some reason, however, Mrs. Shubrick didn't choose to wear the same jewelry to the race, and she did not discover the theft.

In mid-morning, after the Shubricks left the house for the race, the slave girl flew upstairs and lighted a candle and touched it to a lace curtain, then to the canopy on the tester bed, and then to the counterpane. Soon the room was in flames. They won't know anything about the jewels now, she thought, as she flew down the circular stairway.

When the Shubricks returned home, only the first floor of their mansion remained. They stood in the garden and looked at the ruins of their mansion. They were people of strong fiber, however, and they set about at once planning the rebuilding of their home. It would be even more elegant than the first one.

Although the slave girl's crime was never discovered, she was unable to accept the fate of being left on the plantation by the young man whom she had trusted to give her freedom. Although she has not lived for nearly two hundred years, she still walks in the avenue of oaks near the Cooper River. Her spirit believes the young man will return for her.

Note: It is difficult to obtain a pass to get into the Charleston Naval Base and view the trees.

Hilton Head Island

Hilton Head Island, the largest island south of Long Island, New York, is a subtropical 12-mile-long, 5-mile-wide strip of land where you can view forests of moss-draped oaks, palmettoes, Spanish sword and other palmy growth, as well as white, hard-packed sand beaches. The island is approximately 42 square miles in size.

Bordering the pure white beach that meanders around Hilton Head Island are hotels and condominiums. Oaks, veiled in Spanish moss, pines and other huge trees shade the area back from the shore.

The island is located about 30 miles from Savannah, the closest city, and about 90 miles from Charleston. Lying on the Intracoastal Waterway between these two coastal cities, Hilton Head has been connected to the mainland by a bridge since 1956.

History focused on this island several times. On Nov. 7, 1861, a very decisive battle of the Civil War was fought here, the Battle of Port Royal Sound. On that day the federal troops overran the Confederates' Fort Walker on the island's north rim after the Union fleet had knocked out the guns of both Fort Walker and Fort Beauregard. Another eventful war event would take place here before World War II.

But before we leave the age when the production of sea island cotton made millionaires of the planters, some mention should be made of the people who owned large tracts of land on this island. The principal landholders included the Baynards, Chaplins, Draytons, Elliotts, Ficklings, Gardners, Grahams, Jenkinses, Kirks, Lawtons, Mathews, Popes, Seabrooks, Scotts, Stoneys and Stuarts. The exact boundaries of their plantations are disputable since the official land records have been burned.

After the turn of the century, the island, which had been covered with huge plantations, became for the most part a hunting preserve for some wealthy northerners. Their expeditions were interrupted when some 13,000 soldiers and marines landed on the island in the largest amphibious operation attempted by American forces prior to World War II. Fort Walker soon became a large naval base, protected by miles of earthworks and the area became the federal headquarters for the Department of the South. Troops and civilians came to the island, and the population increased to 50,000.

In 1949, Georgia lumberman Fred C. Hack came to have a look at the timber, and the future of Hilton Head Island changed. Hack had unusual vision for the tropical island and imagined the possibilities if the island were developed into a resort. He formed a business partnership with three other Georgians: his father-in-law, C. C. Stebbins, General Joseph B. Fraser, and O. T. McIntosh, Sr. They bought the land for $450,000 and cut enough timber in the first six months to pay for the purchase.

Today Hilton Head Island is one of the nation's most noted resort areas, with such beautiful resort communities as Sea Pines Plantations, Palmetto Dunes, Port Royal Plantation, and Spanish Wells Plantation.

To get to Hilton Head Island, follow U.S. 17 South from Charleston to I-95, then turn onto U.S. 462, which will take you to Highway 278. Highway 278 takes you to and across Hilton Head Island.

The Eliza Tree

Eliza was Sarah Baynard's body servant, and she labored at the plantation house at the time it was purchased by William Baynard. It was about that time, from one streak of suggestion to another, that Sarah had begun to surmise that William was enjoying Eliza's charms. Something more, uh, intimate was going on between the two, and Sarah just knew it! She took it upon herself to find out just what was going on.

One day as evening was about to creep onto Hilton Head Island, Sarah threw her black shawl over her head and left the mansion. She intended to wander along the marshlands for a mile or two and then just happen to return home by way of Eliza's cabin.

At that time Hilton Head Island was a singular place. It consisted of little else than the sea, sand dunes covered with sea oats, cotton plantations, and what seemed to be miles of marshlands and miles of forests. The island was separated from mainland South Carolina by a creek oozing its way through a wilderness of cord grass and slime and shore birds. The route that Sarah chose was scant in growth other than marsh grass, but Eliza's cabin was encircled by large live oaks, draped in Spanish moss.

No one noticed the lovely Sarah as she slowly made her way along the marsh, for it was not her wont to leave her mansion except to travel in her extraordinarily beautiful black carriage. It bore the Baynard coat of arms and was always pulled by four matching black horses.

Even though the stroll was distressing to her due to her mission, it soon took on a kind of joy. In her whole life she had scarcely taken notice of the palmettoes waving in the breeze, the Spanish sword thrusting from the sand, and the erratically growing limbs of live oak, overhanging with gauzy icicles of Spanish moss. It came to her that as she traveled in her carriage, she rarely lifted the lace curtain at the window. The wax myrtle and yaupon holly were not identifiable to her, but their beauty caught her eye. She could identify the wild smilax, for she had used it in decorations at Christmastide.

Before Sarah realized it, it had grown quite late, and the moon had ripened into a fiery orange melon that sauntered above the beach. Quickly, she turned and walked in the direction of the slave cabins.

The birds had gone to roost now, and all was quiet and still as she strolled toward the cabin, moving from behind one oak tree to another. The vegetation that had been thrilling only moments before now became gloomy. The Spanish moss swung gently in the breeze, throwing unexpected shadows on Sarah's face and in her path. Although she was disturbed, she went on, her mission to accomplish. In her solitary walk, she wondered what creatures hunkered down behind each wax myrtle, each yaupon. Was it true what the slaves talked about? Were there such creatures as plat-eye, hags, hants, boo-daddies and ghosts who lived in these woods?

Now a new horror presented itself. What if indeed she saw her husband in the cabin of her maid, Eliza? What would she do? The lovely mistress of the plantation candidly confessed to herself that her feelings were most perplexing and incomprehensible at that moment, but they were still most singular.

It was from a tree such as this island oak that Eliza was hung in a cage.   *Photo by Sid Rhyne*

She kept her eye on the path as she darted from tree to tree.

Eliza's cabin was the first in the double row of small houses. Sarah surmised that Eliza's bedroom would be at the rear, so she pulled her shawl tightly around her head, and quietly walked to the back of the house. A lamp had been lit. Eliza was moving about in the room. Even Sarah at that moment had to admit that the loveliness of Eliza was that of an ancient queen. It was true that she was a maiden artless and innocent in the social graces, but in natural beauty hers was unsurpassed on Hilton Head Island.

Eliza was alone as she prepared for her bed, and Sarah sighed as if a deadly burden had been lifted from her breast. But she couldn't take her eyes off Eliza who now was lifting a thin leg to the back of a chair. She attached to the ankle a gold chain, then swung her leg from the chair. Then, with grace and shapeliness, she swung her other leg to the back of the chair. On that ankle she also placed a chain of gold. As Sarah thought about it, those chains looked for all the world like the two gold chains in her collection. But how in the world could Eliza have come into possession of the chains from Sarah's collection?

Eliza wiggled her lissome figure from her dress. Her figure, as seen by Sarah out in the darkness, was a brazen cloud, floating as though it had known the feel of satin and gold. Just at that very moment, Eliza did something that so stunned Sarah the horror would go with her for the rest of her life. The maiden servant opened the drawer of a rustic chest and removed a chain of gold, richly gleaming in the lamplight. As Eliza held it up, Sarah recognized it as her brooch on a gold chain! How in the world had Eliza gotten her hands on it? The naked Eliza turned, and as the emerald in the brooch caught the light it was like the flash of a sword in Sarah's heart. But her heart was to be stabbed even deeper. Just then, her husband, William, stepped up to Eliza and hooked the clasp of the gold chain at the back of her neck.

So it was true. Sarah's husband was carrying on with the servant girl. And in such an outrageous, ugly, unholy way. To have such a horrid circumstance with the servant girl was one thing, but to steal her jewelry and give it to Eliza was quite another. Sarah rushed home and unlocked the desk in her upstairs bedroom to check on the collection of unusual and valuable jewelry. The brooch and gold chains were not there!

The jewelry had come to her from her father, whose own father had once given it to his favorite slave girl. This was the second time that jewelry had been exchanged for the favors of a servant girl.

Sarah's trembling fingers moved the other jewelry in the velvet-lined box. It was all there. The belt made of gold links, each hooked to another, was in the bottom of the box. A rare, magnificent cross of rubies set in an elaborate gold casing was there, as well as a carved emerald and diamond jabot pin. But the two gold chains and the emerald brooch were missing. "Green ice," her grandfather had called the brooch.

Sarah decided she should have been wearing the jewelry all along. The mannerism to conceal brilliance and achievement behind a conservative facade had been drilled into her by her parents and grandparents. And where had it gotten her?

The following day, Sarah confronted Eliza. Her plan was to get rid of the girl and say nothing to her husband. She'd quietly get the jewelry back, send Eliza away, and perhaps in time, she could bring herself to forgive her husband. She knew she'd never forget what he had done to her. But first things first.

Sarah sucked in her breath and said, "Eliza, I know that you are carrying on with my husband."

"Why all the up and down bout that," the girl sassed. "You don't treat him nice like I do."

The retort surprised Sarah but she didn't let on. She regarded her servant intently and thought she'd never known a more anguished time. Deep emotion was attached to every word.

"What my husband and I feel for each other is no concern of yours," Sarah said, trying to remain calm so that anger would not cloud her judgment. "But the fact that you are now in possession of some of my jewelry concerns both of us."

"It's *mine*," Eliza retorted.

"It is *not* yours," Sarah countered icily. "You are like a child. You will take what is given to you, but the jewelry was only mine to do with whatever I chose. And I would never choose to give it to you."

Eliza's shoulders came up with a start.

Sarah observed her servant single-mindedly. She would never surrender. There was no force under which she would crumble. Sarah couldn't be sure what to do but decided to let it rest for this day. Her jaw sagged when she thought of her husband dillydallying with this simple woman. "Eliza, you will have to leave Hilton Head Island. I'll make arrangements for you to leave and I'll see that you have a place to live. I will not leave you helpless. We'll not speak of this again, but later today I'll go to your cabin and receive the jewelry. Within a week, you will be sent away."

Just as she had said, that afternoon Sarah went to Eliza's cabin and took the jewelry from her. After Sarah left the small house, Eliza went to visit a witchdoctor. She had always believed he could effect a cure or cast a spell more efficiently than any other witchdoctor on the island.

The man's face was wrinkled and worked convulsively. He sat before what he called his altar, a table that was littered with lizard and snake skins, dirt and bones. Eliza told him her story, and when she left his house, which smelled much like a rotten onion, she carried a small cloth bag in her hands.

Eliza arrived at Sarah's house to prepare the evening meal, which was one of her tasks. That night she made deviled crab, a food at which she was an expert at preparing. As she mixed the ingredients for one particular serving, she emptied a few grains of something from the bag she had brought from the witchdoctor's house. Of one thing she was certain: It contained crystals of strychnine. Eliza made sure the crystals went into the crab that would be eaten by Sarah.

As the Baynards sat at the oval table in the dining room, under a Waterford crystal chandelier, Sarah took a bite of her deviled crab. Suddenly she was deathly sick. Her mouth burned, and she clutched her throat. Within minutes she was dead. Eliza was accused of poisoning Sarah.

The people of Hilton Head Island were outraged. They had heard rumors of Eliza's liaisons with Sarah's husband. Everyone knew that William Baynard had given Eliza some of Sarah's jewelry, and they suspected that Sarah had discovered the indiscretion. Also, word had quickly spread that Sarah planned to send Eliza away.

A cage of iron was made by the plantation blacksmith, and it was hung from a limb on a huge live oak tree at Big Gate (the present intersection of Matthews Drive and Marshlands Road.) Eliza was hung within the cage, and her limp body was suspended there for all to see. For many years, the tree on which Eliza was hung was called the Eliza Tree.

Eliza's ghost comes back to the tree where she was hung, forever keeping alive the story of her horrible murder of her mistress.

Note: Turn right off U.S. 278 at Matthews Drive, the site of Zion Cemetery and the Baynard Mausoleum, and go to the intersection of Matthews Drive and Marshlands Road. There is a seafood restaurant at the intersection; also a huge oak tree.

The Unparalleled Rides
of the Late William Baynard

Indeed, phenomena have occurred at the Baynard Plantation Ruins of so completely an unexpected nature, so entirely unusual and off-beat, as to leave no doubt that the place is haunted. There have been many nights that U.S. 278 between the Baynard Plantation Ruins in Sea Pines and the Zion Cemetery and Baynard Mausoleum, located at the intersection of U.S. 278 and Matthews Drive have had the residents in an uproar.

William Edings Baynard (1800-1849) was a nephew of the man who married Sarah Black. This William Baynard inherited Muddy Creek Plantation as well as Spanish Wells Plantation. In 1829 he married Catherine Adelaide Scott, a daughter of prosperous planters who owned Grasslawn Plantation.

William Edings Baynard was a man of firmness, of immovable resolution. And above all, he was a gambler. One night it was conveyed to his soul the idea of playing a poker game whereby the stakes would be the plantations owned by the players. The wonder, the rapturous astonishment of the very suggestion to the other players may be conceived. But Baynard was obstinate. The game would be played at once. When the game was over, Baynard had won Braddock's Point Plantation.

Baynard Plantation Ruins   *Photo by Sid Rhyne*

Ill-fated Col. John Joseph Stoney, the loser, was a great-grandson of Revolutionary War hero Dr. George Mosse. For him it was a night of unusual gloom, but he kept his thoughts and speculations to himself. Great fortunes were lost in games of chance in those days, and as men sat in their game rooms smoking Cuban cigars, their fiece resolute came to the fore, and they'd die before they'd lose their honor. Such a thing as evacuating a game, or even a hurricane for that matter, was alien to them.

In 1849, William Baynard died of yellow fever. He had suffered unutterably, as he lay on the tester bed in an upstairs bedroom of the plantation he had won in the poker game. Now his lifeless body lay there, waiting to be prepared for burial. The face assumed the usual pinched and sunken outline. The lips were of the usual marble paleness. The eyes were lustreless. There was no warmth. Pulsation had ceased.

His burial box was being built to conform with the shape of his body, only larger. The casket was designed in the form of a man, with head, shoulders, hips, legs, feet. The funeral was hastened on account of the rapid advance of what was supposed to be decomposition of the remains.

The funeral cortege moved from Braddock's Point to the Chapel of Ease at the head of Broad Creek where William Baynard was laid to anything-but-rest in his Baynard Mausoleum.

The rector spoke, "I am the resurrection and the life: he that believeth in me, though he were dead, yet shall ye live." Just then a cloud passed overhead, and a few drops of rain fell on the mourners. The rector reached out and caught a few drops of rain. "Let not your hearts be troubled," he said quietly. "The God who sends the rain to nourish the crops and plant life sends the strength to sustain us in our hour of grief. And He will nourish us as we go into eternal life, and whosoever believeth in Him shall not perish, but enter into that eternal life." He paused and let the rain drain from his hand.

The Baynard tomb, like a tiny Greek temple, stood proudly in the cemetery for a little over ten years, and then it was ransacked by Yankee soldiers who had heard that some of the people buried there had been laid to rest wearing fabulous jewelry.

After the Civil War, on a night brightened by moonlight, the black funeral carriage of William Baynard, draped in black just as it had been on the day of his burial, left Braddock's Point Plantation. It moved very slowly over the roadway (today U.S. 278), and it stopped at the gates of each plantation. William Baynard, silvery and ghostly, left the carriage, opened the gates to the plantation, paused, then closed the gates. After he was back in his carriage, he gave the order to the driver, sitting on the box, to continue to the next plantation. As they traveled from one plantation to another, Baynard held his hands over his face. Walking behind the carriage as it crept along was a group of servants, dressed in livery of red plush, trimmed in silver braid.

The specter of the splendid carriage draped in black, with the passenger holding his hands over his face, stopping at the gates of each plantation and followed by a band of faithful servants, has been seen on many moonlit nights, slowly moving from Braddock's Point to the mausoleum at Zion Cemetery. The agony of Baynard's countenance, the convulsive struggle of his frame, gave evidence of superhuman exertion.

Two-foot-thick foundation walls are all that remain of Braddock's Point Plantation House, built around 1800 and acquired in 1840 by William E. Baynard. The foundation is tabby — a unique material composed of oyster shells, sand, lime, and water — which characterizes many of this area's antebellum structures. The Baynard Ruins are located on Baynard Park Road in Sea Pines Plantation. Entrance to Sea Pines carries a daily admission fee of $3.00 per car for those who are not residents or guests.

During World War II, a group of men from Brooklyn were stationed at nearby Camp Dilling, and they were told that the women in the planter families on Hilton Head Island owned fabulous jewelry. On a night of particular revelry, they could restrain themselves no longer, and they went to the mausoleum and desecrated every crypt.

You can go to the mausoleum, standing empty and desolate, at the intersection of U.S. 278 and Matthews Drive. The little Greek temple back in the oaks and magnolias contains the remains of no person.

A historical plaque stands at this intersection:

> Zion Chapel of Ease and Cemetery, a chapel of
> St. Luke's Parish, established May 23, 1767,
> built of wood shortly after 1786 under the
> direction of Captain John Stoney and Isaac
> Fripp, was consecrated in 1833. Members of the
> Barksdale, Baynard, Chaplin, Davant, Fripp,
> Kirk, Matthews, Pope, Stoney, and Webb
> families worshipped here. By 1868 the chapel
> was destroyed.

After you have observed the Baynard Mausoleum, don't fail to look about the old cemetery. One Sally Baynard was buried so long ago that a giant oak tree has tilted her grave marker.

Note: From the entrance to Sea Pines Plantation on U.S. 278, it is 8 miles to the Baynard Ruins, on the right, plainly marked.

Baynard Mausoleum   *Photo by Sid Rhyne*

Daufuskie Island

Daufuskie Island is an undeveloped, primitive island, which is accessible from Hilton Head Island through cruise/tour services that operate out of Harbour Town Yacht Basin and Shelter Cove Harbour. The three-hour tours are offered on a seasonal basis, but charters are available.

Daufuskie Island is a million light years away from the world, happily independent of the hustle and bustle that engrosses the mainland. It is 16 miles from Savannah and can be reached by boat from that city.

For some unknown reason, the author Somerset Maugham was lured to Daufuskie in the early 1940s where he wrote one of his most popular novels, *The Razor's Edge*. If he were to sail into the tiny landing today he'd find it much the same. Natives would be whiling away their long days hacking at roasted oysters.

Three centuries ago, Daufuskie was akin to what it is today except that it was peopled by Indians. There are many legends of this island, including the one that goes like this:

> When a group of men walked through the
> deep woods to a burial ground, where they
> expected to find only the hole in the ground
> where a body had been buried, suddenly the

> sound of a galloping horse rose from the hole
> and disappeared into the woods. Was it a plat-
> eye? they wondered. Plat-eye lived in those
> woods, and that critter could take the shape of
> a horse.

Although four species of poisonous snakes are abundant on this island characterized by luxuriant vegetation, the people who live here ask that any snake that is not threatening a visitor be allowed to live. The island is small, and environmentalists believe that all parts of it are important to its future growth and maintenance, including the snakes. Reptiles, they say, help to control the rodent population. One is advised to be careful when walking, however, and to carry a light after dark. Copperheads are nocturnal and if one should be stepped on the lightning-quick strikes would come fast and furious. Biting and stinging insects also live here, and they seem to come in clouds during the warm summer months. Insect repellents help, especially when dealing with mosquitoes, red bugs, ticks and other varieties. And there's another word of caution from the islanders: Don't kick ant hills. Should you do so, you will surely learn where fire ants got their name.

Daufuskie Island has been spelled Dewfoskey, D'Awfoskee, Dawfuskie, and so forth. The channel between Hilton Head Island and Daufuskie is designated as Dawfuskie River and as Daufuskie Sound on several early maps. It is now called Calibogue Sound.

Daufuskie's Big Foot

While the sun sinks rapidly to rest and ebbing tides retreat round Daufuskie Island, one's imagination might summon thoughts of Big Foot, said to make its way slowly about the darkness of this place so remote it can only be reached by boat.

Big Foot has been called other names: Abominable Snowman, Yeti and, in Florida, Big Ape. By whatever name he answers, he brings to those who know something of his whereabouts sheer terror.

There was a Big Foot who lived in the high Himalayas. His tracks were recorded, his voice heard, his shape photographed.

From the forests of the American Rockies came tales of a Big Foot. He romped in snow and ice and kept a few miles ahead of his hunters.

Indians have accounted for over a thousand sightings, and white trappers and hunters have given depositions, produced photographs, and have made casts of tracks. Still, there are skeptics who believe that the possibility of a huge primate lurking in the woods of civilized areas is inconceivable. Some researchers declare that the northwestern Big Foot is a most extraordinary hoax.

From the high elevations of Nepal, in the vicinity of Mt. Everest, to the ridges of the Rockies and Sierras of the American West, to the swamps of South Carolina, Big Foot is said to have been sighted. Sophisticated efforts have been made to trap him, but to no avail. If indeed he exists, he is obviously endowed with a degree of intelligence that surpasses the technology of human efforts to trap him.

Howard Farmer, John Morgan and Wayne Edwards got an eyeful of the hairy beast hopping through the marshes at Moss Creek Plantation, adjacent to U.S. 278 just before you cross the bridge to enter Hilton Head Island. The next day the men returned to search for Big Foot, but he was not to be found. Big Foot has been sighted on Daufuskie Island, and it is now generally believed that he makes his home there. People who live on Daufuskie don't speak of "if" Big Foot appears, but "when."

On Daufuskie there are no telephones, and the only communication is provided by shortwave radio. The islanders are unruffled, calm. They are not prosperous, but they are contented on their island that is one hour by boat from Savannah. There is one store on the island, but one is enough to serve the residents.

All of the hunters who have tracked Big Foot agree on one thing: He has a certain cunning. And what better environment could he choose for his home than Daufuskie?

The ancient lighthouse at Daufuskie Island

Courtesy of the Daufuskie Company

Savannah

Savannah, on Georgia's seacoast, is where the state began. The founder was Gen. James Oglethorpe, who came to this place with his group of 125 English settlers in 1773. Oglethorpe sailed up the Savannah River some ten miles to a crescent of high land and said, "I have laid out a town."

During the last century, Savannah grew and prospered with the production of cotton. Millions of tons pass through the factoring houses on the Savannah riverfront each year.

In 1955 a grand renewal of the historic section was begun. The Historic Savannah Foundation was formed. This Foundation is a nonprofit membership organization whose principal charges are the preservation of the city's architectural heritage and unique town plan.

Historic old homes and other buildings were purchased and resold. The new owners are restricted under covenants that require them to restore the exteriors in harmony with the architectural heritage of each structure.

And something new is off and running — The Great Savannah Exposition. The multimedia history orientation center will be located in Savannah's Battlefield Park just behind the Savannah Visitors Center in the old Central of Georgia train station. Construction has begun on the multimedia center. Parsons-Brinckerhoff Development Group, the developers of the project, says it will be completed in December, 1985. The center will provide visitors a journey into Savannah's past and into the character and culture of its people.

Visitors to this port city will want to stroll on River Street and Bay Street, both of which run parallel with the Savannah River.

From Hilton Head Island follow U.S. 278, turn onto S.C. 46, and travel to S.C. 170, which you will travel until you connect with U.S. 17 South.

Savannah's
Sweetheart of Mankind

For 44 years, year in and year out, the favorite game of people traveling into the Savannah harbor was to wave to the lovely girl standing in front of her home on Elba Island, near the lighthouse. By day she waved a white apron and by night she waved a lantern; it was rare indeed if anyone traveling that way didn't get a friendly wave. Where else in the world do you get friendliness like this? the seamen asked. Where else in the world? But Florence Martus was not flapping her apron in the breeze only to bear goodwill. She truly hoped that one of the seamen would be her fiance, who had sailed away and promised to return to her.

Sometime in the late nineteenth century, she bade farewell to her fiance as he sailed away. She made a solemn promise that she would greet every ship that passed the lighthouse until he returned. He would see her as he sailed by, and he would know that she had waited for him. Each time a vessel approached, she ran from the house in her flat-heeled, two-button shoes, holding her apron high in the air. All hands on board waved back, and some of them called greetings to her. But each ship passed by, going on down the river. Her face did not change expression. Perhaps the next vessel . . .

"Waving Girl" statue greets ships in Savannah, Georgia, harbor
. . . Florence Martus stood by the river to greet every ship
entering the Savannah harbor from 1887 until her death in
1931, thus earning her name as the "Waving Girl." Today this
statue stands as a symbol of hospitality to world freighters and
land visitors alike.   *Credit: Savannah Area Convention and Visitors Bureau*

During this time, and well into the twentieth century, the only transportation to and from the islands between Charleston, Beaufort and Savannah was by boat. There were boats of all sizes and descriptions, and their cargo usually consisted of potatoes, cabbages, tobacco, beef, corn and wheat. And, of course, sea island cotton. The cotton was bound into long, narrow bales. When the vessels left the dock, they carried a cargo of Low Country products.

Some of the boats had upper and lower decks, and even staterooms. The larger and more expensive boats had two beds in each stateroom. Most of the officers on the ships, like the purser, captain and engineer, had wives in Charleston or Beaufort or Savannah. But they blew their whistles at the girl waving her apron. They all loved her, for no person could ever be more friendly or faithful.

And there was always a fishing fleet that went out at first light and came in at dusk. Like a swarm of flies, the small boats swarmed into the harbor, jib and mainsail out, men on deck, whacking away with blades that flashed in the light as they cleaned the day's catch. Seagulls swarmed overhead, screaming for a morsel. Occasionally a sea turtle was on board. When properly cooked, sea turtle was delicious, as were their eggs. Turtle stew was a favorite with seamen.

Florence waved to every ship that passed Elba Island, and she learned the ways of the sea. She created her own little weather station, becoming a student of clouds, wind, surf and sun. She became an expert on predicting weather patterns. One day all of the signs indicated a terrible hurricane was about to crash on Elba Island. It was likely that the water level would rise to an astonishing level. Although the sun was shining and the sky was clear, Florence spoke to her brother of an impending storm. She decided that when the storm came she would take refuge about halfway up the spiral stairway in an abandoned fort on the island. By the next morning, dark clouds scudded over the sea, and ships were listing in the waves, which were getting higher and higher.

As time passed, the wind blew water so furiously it appeared to be a white froth. Hunks of foam flew through the air. No ships were in sight, so Florence went to the abandoned fort and took her station midway up the spiral stairway. The wind became so swift and strong that no man could have walked in it. The water swept over the bank and began to rise. Florence held tightly to the stairway and prayed that God would let her live at least until her fiance returned. Finally, the wind quietened, and the water began to recede. The storm was over.

Occasionally a ship would dock at Elba Island, and Florence would run down to the dock and speak to the hands. She listened to their talk for hours on end, catching snatches of conversation coming from several groups of seamen who talked at the same time. She never heard a word that concerned her fiance. But that didn't deter her from waving to every boat that passed her little house on Elba Island, 7 1/2 miles below Savannah.

The vigil ended in 1931 when Florence's brother retired from his government job as lighthouse keeper. He had reached the age of 70 and had been the lighthouse keeper since 1887. He and his sister moved away.

In 1938 the Propellor Club had a celebration in honor of Florence. Over 3,000 people attended. A huge birthday cake was decorated with a replica of her home where she had lived on Elba Island. Many state officials attended the celebration, and they chose a fitting title for Florence, whom they had always referred to as the "Sweetheart of Mankind."

A progressive harbor has evolved since the time of Florence Martus, but you can see the statue of Florence waving her apron, her dog at her side, on River Street in Savannah. A plaque by the statue reads:

Florence Martus
1869 - 1943
Savannah's Waving Girl

On another side of the statue, the following words are inscribed:

Her immortality stems from her
friendly greeting to passing ships,
a welcome to strangers entering the
port and a farewell to wave them
safely onward.

The sculpture is by Felix De Weldon, done in 1971.
If you take a cruise and pass Elba Island, gaze devoutly at the island. The waving girl is said to appear from time to time, always waving her apron, trusting that her fiance will return to her.

The Ghost at the Pirates' House

Savannah's famous Pirates' House Restaurant stands on one of the most historical spots in Georgia. Here, Trustees' Garden, the first public agricultural experimental garden in America, was located. The garden was modeled very closely after the Chelsea Botanical Garden in London, a diagram of which hangs in the Jolly Roger Room of the restaurant. (Source: From brochure by Pirates' House host, Herb Traub.)

The first building constructed on the former garden was an inn for visiting seamen. The inn was only a block from the Savannah River, and pirates — with bright scarves tied around their heads, holding a gun and sometimes clinching a knife between their teeth — often stormed in and demanded the fiery grog served there. Today there are 23 fascinating dining rooms in the Pirates' House, and to visit Savannah and not have a meal in one of them is almost sinful. Any room in which you dine has probably seen the likes of adventurers from Singapore or Shanghai.

But the ghost of the Pirates' House hangs out in the Captain's Room. 'Tis said he's the spirit of old Cap'n Flint, from Robert Louis Stevenson's book *Treasure Island.* You'll even see some ancient pages from a very rare edition of that book on the walls

The famous Pirates' House, 20 East Broad Street, Savannah. A
Savannah Landmark.   *Photo Courtesy Herb Traub*

of this room. And don't miss the ceiling beams, which are hand hewn and joined with wooden pegs. Old Cap'n Flint, who originally buried the notorious treasure on Treasure Island, died in this very room. His trusted first mate, Billy Bones, was at his side when he raised up on an elbow and rasped, "In the name of God, I am Cap'n Flint," then fell back and breathed his last breath.

Some of the waiters refuse to go into this room when old Cap'n Flint is cutting up, such as making sounds, musical yet sad, casting shadows, vague and unsteady, and rattling dishes. But this is not the only legend connected with this place.

Stories are still whispered of a tunnel extending from the old Rum Cellar to the river, through which drunken men were carried back to their vessels. Many was the time a sailor awoke after a night at the Pirates' House to find himself on a vessel bound for a port in the opposite direction from his destination.

The validity of the Pirates' House has been recognized by the American Museum Society, and this historic tavern is an authentic house museum. The property was acquired by the Savannah Gas Company in 1948. Mrs. Hansell Hillyer, who is endowed with extraordinary imagination and talent, transformed the fascinating old museum into its present use as a restaurant.

In addition to the 23 dining rooms, be sure you don't overlook the picturesque little outdoor patio where a huge old anchor and wishing well will catch your eye. The wishing well bucket is over a hundred years old.

The splendid paintings exhibited throughout are by Savannah's leading artists. And take the time to browse in the gift shop, even if old Cap'n Flint is cutting up.

Note: The Pirates' House Restaurant is located at 20 East Broad at Bay Street, one block from the river. You can't miss it as you drive along Bay Street. If ever a building looked like a pirate's house, this is it.

The Ghost of
Mr. Habersham

If ever a home is a bouquet, full-fruited in summer, blossom-scented in spring, and berried and candle-scented in winter, it's the Habersham home in Savannah, now known as the Olde Pink House Restaurant and Tavern. The kitchen air is savory with the fragrance of plum pudding or fruit cake, buttery cookies and, best of all, duck.

The Pink House, known as Savannah's most elegant and gracious setting, is where regional foods are served with old colonial flavor, charm and southern hospitality.

Consider an authentically furnished dining room, with crystal chandelier, fine antique paintings and candlelight, and a meal consisting of Black Turtle Bean Soup, Salmagundi, homemade yeast puff rolls and an entree of fresh crab, all prepared in a most delightful southern manner. To finish off such a meal, it would be outlandish not to select a dessert and praline coffee.

But there's more. The charming building comes with a ghost who is none other than Mr. Habersham himself. And he is quite entertaining. You see, this man was never known for his modesty. What he set out to do, he did. And when he sets out to entertain you as a spirit, he does.

The elegant Habersham house was built on land granted by

The Olde Pink House, Savannah. Only 18th century mansion in Georgia. Built in 1771 for James Habersham, Jr.

Courtesy of the Savannah Morning News

the Crown, and it opened in 1771. It wasn't only the talk of Savannah, it was noted even in Europe for its symmetry and beauty. Of the many rooms in the mansion, one room was set aside as a conference room. Some secret meetings held there helped secure the independence of the colonies. The Habersham home became as much an enclave for high society as a home for the Habershams. It was the perfect place to linger, to mingle, to be entertained. You never had to look very far to find somebody with a royal title.

By 1811 the soft native brick began to bleed through the plastered walls and mysteriously changed the color of Habersham House from white to Jamaican pink, and that is when it picked up the name Pink House.

In 1811 the Pink House became the Planters Bank, the first bank in the state of Georgia, and housed the monies of all the colonists in the vicinity. Massive cast-iron vaults with dungeonlike doors are still there today, but they are used as wine cellars.

In 1865, during Sherman's march to the sea, the halls of Habersham were opened to military generals, and General York set up headquarters in the pink mansion. After the Civil War, the property changed hands many times, and it was used as an office building, bookstore and colonial tea room.

When the Habersham house was restored to its former elegance and transformed into a restaurant, James Habersham, Jr. came home to enjoy. He's having a ball, but let those who know him tell of it:

Gloria Nanfria, the friendliest of ladies, will meet you at the elegant front door. As we entered, gazing wide-eyed at the beauty of the house, I quickly asked about the ghost. "Mr. Habersham is very particular about how his house is operated," Gloria begins. "It's run in precisely the manner he desires. And since he never lived in this house during the hot summer months, he only is active from October to Spring."

By now we're seated at a round table, covered with pink linen tablecloth and set with fine china, crystal and silverware. Bonnie Gueller comes over to the table and picks up the conversation. "I work down in the tavern, and many times when I light a candle, and Mr. Habersham doesn't want that candle lighted, the flame will go out. On the other hand, some candles just flame up, by themselves."

"Do these things *really* happen?" we ask.

"Many times! Bill Royal knows all about it," says Bonnie, motioning for Bill Royal to come to the table. "There is no question in my mind that Mr. Habersham is a very important part of this restaurant," he says. "Sometimes I feel a very cold draft of air pass by me, and I know who it is. He's here that night."

"Has anyone actually seen Mr. Habersham?" we ask.

"Just you wait," Gloria says as she heads in the direction of the kitchen. When she returns, a cook, Rebecca, is with her.

"Rebecca, have you seen the ghost?"

"I've seen Mr. Habersham several times, and he's always watching me cook. Sometimes, when I'm standing at the stove, I have a strange feeling, and two times I whirled around and there he was, watching me."

"Well, he must approve of your food. It's absolutely delicious," I answered.

"If you didn't like it, he'd let me know," Rebecca says, going back toward the kitchen.

As Gloria, Bonnie and Bill talk, we learn that gas fireplace logs suddenly are lighted by themselves, and candles that haven't been touched, flame up, and that at least once the bartender has felt Mr. Habersham's hand on his shoulder.

"He's very curious, not mean at all," Gloria says. "And he has his favorites. When he's here there are some employees whom he constantly picks at. Others, he lets alone. And, oh yes, I almost forgot to tell you that on occasion one of the chandeliers will swing from one side to another. For no reason at all."

"Does he ever come here after the restaurant has been closed for the night?"

"Mercy, yes," Gloria quickly answers. "Some mornings we come to work and all of the candles on the tables and in the windows have burned down to the candleholders. And we'd never in the world leave this house at night with a candle burning!"

We look at the friendly group who've told us about Mr. Habersham and ask them if they'd ever stay in the house at night, alone.

"Never! No way!"

Note: The Olde Pink House Restaurant and Tavern is located at 23 Abercorn on Reynolds Square, just around the corner from Bay Street.

17 Hundred 90

Chris Jurgenson is America's answer to Dudley Moore, the talented, winsome English actor. Jurgenson has the same knock-dead smile, English accent, aura of success and besides that he owns one of Savannah's most splendid restaurants 17 Hundred 90.

Jurgenson sits in a plush chair in his handsome office and says, candidly, "I don't believe in ghosts." Without further ado, he continues, "Our ghost here is friendly. She's *very* friendly. Now there's a ghost I know about on a plantation out on the river, and that's a vicious ghost. He kills people. But our ghost is nice."

17 Hundred 90 has guest rooms that can be rented as well as rooms for dining. Everyone who enters the door of the tall, white structure gets special treatment. That's just the way Jurgenson wants it, and that's just the way he is. You have the feeling that if you had a problem, he'd be the first to help you out.

Jurgenson went to school in England, where he had his first encounter with a supernatural being. "Something appeared on the bottom of the stairs. A bunch of hunting dogs were kept in the building, and they all went berserk."

Shortly after that, Jurgenson came to Savannah and bought the building where his restaurant is located. The year was 1976.

17 Hundred 90 in the heart of the historic district of Savannah.

Credit: John G. Smith Associates

"The building was only one room, and a burned-out shell," he says. "It had been empty for decades. And the previous owner told me about weird movements on Sundays. Only on Sundays. Empty rocking chairs would rock, things like that.

"I did my work here on Sundays and soon discovered that unusual, unexplainable things did happen on Sundays. Things like toilets flushing where no toilets existed."

"Who is the ghost?" we asked.

"Her name is Anna Powell. Anna was in love with a German sailor, and obviously her love was not returned, for she jumped from the top of this house and killed herself. It seems that when I, of German descent, bought the house, she became really exuberant. But then she quietened down, and for two years we heard nothing from her.

"And then one day some ladies came here looking for a room for the night. When they entered the bedroom upstairs, one of them said she was psychic. She leaned her head against a wall and was very quiet for a moment, meditating, I suppose. Then she said, 'You've had a ghost here. In this very room. She liked it here, but she likes it even more in her new home.'

"That really startled me," Jurgenson said, "and I asked her if she knew where Anna's new home is.

"The psychic said that all she could tell me was that Anna had moved into a home located adjacent to a lake.

"All of the hair on the back of my neck stood up," Jurgenson said. "I had just moved into a house adjacent to a lake."

"Have you encountered Anna?" we asked.

"No. But some of my friends have. Once, I went to Berlin and let friends live in my house while I was gone. They called me in Berlin. They said there were weird happenings in the house. The whole house had taken on a kind of macabre atmosphere. They couldn't stand it, so they moved out.

"Then, a year or so later, I went back to Berlin. And I let other friends use my home while I was away. They, too, called me in Berlin and wanted to know if strange things happened in my house, unusual movements of furniture, strange noises. Before I had an opportunity to answer them, they said, 'We're leaving this place right now!' "

17 Hundred 90 is located in the heart of Savannah's Historic District. It's a unique jewel in this collection of outstanding architectural treasures. The 14 beautifully appointed guest rooms provide guests with unexpected touches of Old South charm. And Jurgenson points out that Anna doesn't live here anymore.

Gourmet Magazine calls 17 Hundred 90 Savannah's most elegant dining room. The whole place is elegant, intriguing, exquisite. You'll go away believing that if ever a young man could come here from England and take one room and a shell of an old building and transform it into a combination of inn, restaurant and lounge that's nationally noted, Chris Jurgenson would be the one person who could do it. And he did.

Note: 17 Hundred 90 is located on Lincoln Street, off Bay Street, in the Historic District.

Epilogue

You have just finished reading the tales on the stretch of land that I believe is richer in folklore than any other. Normal? Not by any stretch of the imagination. Rice was grown from the Cape Fear River near Wilmington to Savannah, and the rice planters were millionaires. They lived a lifestyle that is almost inconceivable to us today. To live the life of this gilded age required a tremendous labor force, for which slaves were brought to this coast from Africa. With them came unusual and charming superstitions, customs and beliefs, many of which are common today in this coastal area. And therein lies the characteristics that distinguish the sliver of coast from Wilmington to Savannah from similar havens.

Index

Adam-style architecture, 135
Africa, 185
All Saints Church, 52, 53, 69
Allston, John, 63
Allston, Joseph, 63
Alston, Aaron Burr, 63
Alston, Governor Joseph, 61, 63
Alston, Prince, 114, 115, 116
Alston, Sue, 112, 114
Alston, Will, 106, 108, 112
Alston, William, 135
American Colonies, 87
American Museum Society, 173
American Revolution, 83, 87, 92, 117
Anglican Church, 119
Arabian Nights, 79
Ashley River, 117, 119
Atlantic Ocean, 17, 47, 117

Bank of Charles Town, 122
Barksdale family, 153
Battery, the, 117, 118, 130
Baynard, Sarah, 141–47, 149
Baynard, William, 141, 149
Baynard, William E., 152
Baynard, William Edings, 149, 151, 152
Baynard Mausoleum, 151, 152, 153

Baynard Park Road, 152
Baynard Plantation Ruins, 149, 152, 153
Baynards, the, 140, 147, 153
Beaufort, S,C., 9, 167
Beauregard, Gen. Pierre Gustave Toutant de, 127, 129, 130, 131
Belin, Rev. James L., 56
Belvidere, 134, 135, 136
Big Ape, 157
Big Foot, 157, 158
Big Gate, 147
Black River, 85, 87
Blaskey family, 93
Blaskey, S. T., 93, 94, 96, 97
Blockade Runner Museum, 17
Boney, 121, 122, 123, 124, 125
Bootsie, 78, 79, 80
Boston Red Sox, 99
Braddocks Point Plantation, 149, 151, 152
Broad Creek, 151
Broad Street (Charleston), 127, 130, 131
Broad Street (Georgetown), 85, 90
Broad Street (Savannah), 173
Brookgreen Gardens, 66, 67, 70
Brookgreen Plantation, 56, 67, 70
Browne, Sir Thomas, 79

Bryan, 71, 73, 74, 75

Burgwin-Wright House, 38

Burr, Aaron, 61, 63, 64, 65, 66

Burr, Theodosia, 61, 63, 64, 65, 66

Burroughs, Adeline Cooper, 47

Caesar, 78, 122

Calibogue Sound, 156

Calhoun, John C., 125

Camp Dilling, 153

Cape Fear River, 17, 35, 38

Carolina Beach, 18

Cato, Rev., 67

Central of Georgia, 163

Chandler, 56, 58, 59

Chandler's Wharf, 17

Chaplins, the, 140, 153

Charles, 78, 79, 80

Charleston, 51–53, 117–18, 167;
    Belvidere Plantation, 133–38; City
    Hall, 127–31; St. Philips Church and
    graveyard, 119–25

Charleston City Hall, 127, 131

Charleston Country Club, 135

Charleston horse racing, 135

Charleston Museum, 58, 59

Charleston Naval Base, 133, 135, 138

Charlestonians, 117

Charles Town, 117, 119, 121, 122

Chattanooga, 43

Chelsea Botanical Garden, 171

Christmas legend of the animals,
    114–16

Church Street (Charleston), 123, 124

City Gazette & Daily Advertiser, 134

Civil War: and Baynard Mausoleum, 152;
    Gen. Gustave Toutant de Beauregard
    (CSA), 127–31; and Hagley Planta-
    tion, 78, 83; and Hilton Head Island,
    139; and Olde Pink House Restau-
rant (Habersham house), 177; and
    Wilmington, 17–18

Cooper River, 117, 118, 123, 133, 135,
    138

Confederacy, 124

Confederate Company A (Tenth S.C.
    Rifle Guards), 78–79

Cornwallis, 38

Daufuskie Island, 155–56, 157–59

Daufuskie Sound, 156

Davant family, 153

Dawfuskie River, 156

Delavillete, Mr., 91

Deslonde, Caroline, 129

Detroit Tigers, 99

Diptheria, 59

Dolly, 79

Draytons, the, 140

Duncan, Tom, 70

Edwards, Wayne, 158

Elba Island, 44, 165–69

Eliza, 141–47

Elliotts, the, 140

Elmwood Cemetery, 93, 94, 97

England, 78, 91, 117, 121, 182

Estill, 10

Eugene, 77–82

Farmer, Howard, 158

Ferry schedule (Fort Fisher to South-
    port), 18

Ficklings, the, 140

Flagg family, 51, 67, 70

Flagg, Alice, 49–53, 56

Flagg, Allard, 49, 51, 52, 56

Flagg, J. Ward, 67, 68, 69, 70

Flint, Captain, 171–73

Fort Beauregard, 139
Fort Fisher, 18, 39, 41, 43
Fort Fisher Civil War Museum, 39
Fort Fisher Marine Resources Center, 18, 40
Fort Fisher Historic Site and Museum, 18
Fort Sumter, 130
Fort Walker, 139, 140
Fourth Street (Wilmington), 38
Fraser, Gen. Joseph B., 140
Fripp family, 153
Fripp, Isaac, 153
Front Street (Georgetown), 85
Fulton, Edwin O., 55–59
Fulton, Edwin O., Jr., 59

Gabriel, 79
Gardners, the, 140
Gause family, 21
General Assembly, 134
Georgetown, 47, 66, 77, 83, 85; S. T. Blaskey of, 93–97; and Francis Marion, 87–92; Tom Yawkey Wildlife Center, 99–103
Georgetown County, 135
Glen, Governor, 134
Grahams, the, 140
Grand Strand, 47, 49
Grasslawn Plantation, 149
Great Savannah Exposition, 163
Green, Dr. Samuel, 37
Gueller, Bonnie, 178
Gulf Stream, 47

Habersham, James, Jr., 175, 176, 177, 178, 179
Habershams, the, 177
Habersham House, 177
Hack, Fred, 140

Hagley Estates, 82
Hagley Landing, 77
Hagley Plantation, 77, 78, 79, 80, 82
Hamilton, Alexander, 63, 65
Hammock Shop, 83
Hampton Plantation, 105–106; Christmas legend, 113–16; Hampton ghost, 107–12
Hampton Plantation State Park, 10, 106, 112
Harbour Town Yacht Basin and Shelton Cove Harbour, 155
Harrill, George E., 44
Heaven's Gate Church, 74
Hector, 78
Hermit Bunker, 40, 41
Hermit, the, 39–44
Hermitage, The, 49, 52
Heyward, DuBose, 125
Highmarket Street (Georgetown), 85, 90
Hillyer, Mrs. Hansell, 173
Hilton Head Island, 10, 139–140; William Baynard legend, 149–54; Eliza Tree, 141–47
Historic Savannah Foundation, 163
Hobbs, Eliza, 37
Hobbs, Joel, 37
Home by the River, 105
Horry, Ben, 70
Horry, Daniel, 105, 107, 109
Horry, Harriott, 105, 109, 110, 111
Hostler, Alexander, 33, 35, 36, 37
Huguenots, 195
Hume Plantation, 101
Hunter's License Bill, 95
Huntington, Anna, 68
Huntington, Archer, 68
Huntington Beach State Park, 66, 67, 70, 71, 75
Hurricane Hazel, 43

Indian skulls, 55
Indians (Eastern Siouan: Winyahs, Waccamaws), 56
Intracoastal Waterway, 101, 102, 103, 139

Jack, 78
Jenkinses, the, 140
Jocelyn, Samuel R., 33, 36, 37
Johnson, Gov. Robert, 134
Josephine, 79
Joshua, 74
Joyner, Robert L., 103
Jurgenson, Chris, 182–84

Kell, Dr., 36, 37
King Street (Georgetown), 85, 171
King's Road, 73
Kirks, the, 140, 153
Kure Beach, 18

Lafayette, Marquis de, 109
Lawtons, the, 140
Lincoln Street (Savannah), 184
Litchfield Plantation, 57, 78
Lydia, 90

McIntosh, O. T., Sr., 140
McIntyre, Miss Addie, 71
McLaren Mill, 122
Magnolia Island, 67
Manigault, Gabriel, 134
Mansfield Plantation, 91
Marboug, Elenore Marie Florimonde de Fay La Tour, 109
Marion, Francis, 87–92, 105
Market Street (Wilmington), 18, 19, 22, 23, 38
Marshlands Road (Hilton Head Island), 147

Martin family, 31, 32
Martin, John, 25, 26, 28, 29, 30, 31
Martin, Margaret Crawford, 32
Martin, Nancy (Nance), 25, 26, 28, 29, 30, 32
Martin, Silas H., 26, 28, 29, 30, 31
Martus, Florence, 165, 166, 167, 168, 169
Mary, 79
Matthewses, the, 140, 153
Matthews Drive (Hilton Head Island), 147, 153
Maugham, Somerset, 155
May River, 9
Mississippian Period (remains at Wachesaw Plantation), 55–60
Mitchell, Robert, 107, 108
Moliere, 79
Morgan, John, 158
Moore, Dudley, 181
Moss Creek Plantation, 158
Mosse, Dr. George, 151
Muddy Creek Plantation, 149
Murray, Dr. John, 135
Murrells Inlet, 49–53, 55–60
Myrtle Beach, 10, 47, 102

Nanfria, Gloria, 177–79
Nautical Museum, 17
New Hanover County, 17
New Hanover County Museum, 18
Norris, Dr., 59
Nutt, Sarah, 37

Oaks, The, 63, 66
Oakdale Cemetery, 31, 32
Oglethorpe, Gen. James, 163
Old Cotton Exchange, 17
Old Market, 118

Old Town, 119

Olde Pink House Restaurant and Tavern, 175–79

Oyster Point, 119

Palmetto Dunes, 140

Parsons-Brinkerhoff Development Group, 163

The Patriot, 66

Pawleys Island, 9, 10, 53, 77–83

Pee Dee River, 85, 87

Phyllis, 79

Pickens, Governor, 130

Pickens, Lucy Holcombe, 129

Pinckney, Charles, 105

Pinckney, Eliza, 105, 109

Pinckney, Harriott, 105, 107, 109

Pirate's House, 171–73

Popes, the, 140, 153

Port Royal Plantation, 140

Powell, Anna, 183

Planters Bank, 177

Pretty Woods, the (Hampton Plantation), 114

Price-Gause House, 21

Prince, 78

Prince Frederick Pee Dee Episcopal Church, 83

Prince George Winyah Episcopal Church, 83, 85, 90

Prince Street (Georgetown), 85

Propellor Club, 168

Proprietorial Era, 135

Queen Street (Georgetown), 85

Rachel, 79

Razor's Edge, The, 155

Rebecca, 178

Reynolds Square, 179

Rice cultivation, 185

River Street (Savannah), 164, 168

Royal Baking Powder, 95

Royal, Bill, 178

Rum Cellar, 173

Rutledge family, 109, 112

Rutledge, Archibald, 106, 107, 113, 114, 115, 116

Rutledge, Edward, 125

Rutledge, Frederick, 105, 110

Rutledge, John Henry, 108, 110, 111, 112

St. James Church, 19, 33, 36, 38

St. Luke's Parish, 153

St. Mary's Chapel, 79

St. Michael's Episcopal Church, 119, 127, 130

St. Philips Episcopal Church, 119, 121, 123, 124, 125

Sampit River, 85, 87, 99

Savannah, 163–64; Florence Martus, the Waving Girl, 165–69; Old Pink House Restaurant, 175–79; Pirate's House, 171–73; 17 Hundred 90 ghost, 181–84

Savannah Gas Co., 173

Savannah Historic District, 184

Savannah River, 163, 164, 171

Savannah's Battlefield Park, 163

Savannah's Visitor Center, 163

S. C. Historical and Genealogical Magazine, 134

S. C. Ports Authority dock (Georgetown), 85

S.C. Wildlife and Marine Resources Dept., 99

Scott, Catherine Adelaide, 149

Scotts, the, 140

Screven Street (Georgetown), 85

Seabrooks, the, 140

Sea island cotton, 140
Sea Pines Plantation, 140, 149, 152, 153
Seaside Golf Capital, 47
Shakespeare, 79
Sherman, 177
Shubrick, Thomas, 134, 135
Shubricks, the, 135, 136, 137
Slavery, 185
South Island Road (Georgetown), 99
Southport, 18
South Santee River, 105, 109
Spanish Wells Plantation, 140, 149
Stebbins, C. C., 140
Stevenson, Robert Louis, 171
Stoney, Col. John Joseph, 151, 153
Stoneys, the, 140, 153
Stuarts, the, 140
Susanna, 79
Swamp Fox, 87–92, 105
"Sweetheart of Mankind," 168
Swinton, William, 85

Taylor, Wm. Marcus School, 43
Tenth South Carolina Rifle Guards, 78
Traub, Herb, 171
Treasure Island, 171, 173
Trustees' Garden, 171
Tucker, Natalie, 77, 80, 82
Tuckers, the, 78

United Daughters of Confederacy, 18
United States Bank, 122
University of South Carolina, 60

Wacca Wache Marina, 60
Waccamaw Neck, 61, 77
Waccamaw region, 56
Waccamaw River, 57, 59, 60, 79, 82, 85, 87, 122
Wachesaw Plantation, 49, 55, 56, 57, 58, 59, 60
Wachesaw Plantation Limited Partnership, 60
Wachesaw skulls, 55
Ward, Joshua, 56
Ward, Penelope Bentley, 56
Washington, George, 105
Webb family, 153
Wedgefield Plantation, 87, 88, 89, 91
Weldon, Felix D., 169
Weston, Emily, 79
Weston, Plowden, 78, 79
Westons, the, 78
Willcox, Clarke A., 53
Wilmington, 17–18, 25–32, 33–38
Wilmington Chamber of Commerce, 19, 21
Wilmington Historic District, 19
Wilmington Star, The, 23
Winyah Bay, 85, 87
World War II, 39, 140, 153

Yawkey, Tom, 99, 101
Yawkeys, the, 101
Yawkey Wildlife Center, 99, 103
York, General, 177

Zion Cemetery, 147, 152, 153